Praise for *Boyhood Reimagined*

"*Boyhood Reimagined* is the book I wish had existed when I was coming into my own as both a queer person and a parent. In a moment when our rights and families feel more precarious than ever, Ada Malone and Gail Marlene Schwartz have gathered a deeply necessary collection of voices—queer moms raising sons with the radical hope that we can reshape masculinity from within. These essays and conversations don't offer easy answers, but they illuminate the daily, intentional work of raising boys who can resist patriarchy rather than perpetuate it. With honesty, tenderness, and an unflinching awareness of the challenges ahead, this book offers solidarity and inspiration to anyone invested in building a better future. It's a must-read."

— Jessi Hempel, author of *The Family Outing*

"In a world where mirrors and windows can change and save lives, *Boyhood Reimagined* provides an honest and uplifting look into the lives of queer moms raising sons told in their own funny, feisty, and loving voices. Editors Ada Malone and Gail Marlene Schwartz have done a great service in gathering these essays like a bouquet for readers so that queer families can see they are not alone, and heteronormative families can recognize the universalities of parents wanting their children to flourish. In a world where too many boys are encouraged to harden themselves to empathy and dominate others using slurs and physical attacks, this book offers compelling portraits of families that live their belief that caring and supporting others is the truest sign of strength, lighting a way to a vision of a happier and more hopeful future for us all."

— Nancy Churnin, award-winning author of *Rainbow Allies, the True Story of Kids Who Stood Against Hate*

"'Raising boys is indeed the ultimate act of feminist defiance,' writes one lesbian mom in *Boyhood Reimagined*; this collection is full of such gems—the kind of intimate, thoughtful writing I wished for as a lesbian mom coming out when my son was a pre-teen. While some pieces deal with 'typical' parenting challenges through a lesbian lens (like an emotionally sensitive boy for whom the world can be intensely overwhelming, or the juggling act of single-parenting), other essays address concerns about the effect of a profoundly patriarchal culture on a male child of lesbians, providing male role models, or homophobia in schools. At the core of each piece, I hear the underlying heartbeat: I want my son to be a good person. The earned wisdom and honest reflections in this collection will inform and hearten many lesbian parents."

— Deborah A. Miranda, author of *Bad Indians: A Tribal Memoir* and *Sovereign Erotics: A Collection of Two-Spirit Literatures*

"What does it look like to raise boys without traditional, cis male fathers? Amazing and limitless! What is the world coming to? The best yet. A book like this has always been deeply necessary, but especially now, as retrograde viewpoints—the last sulphurous gasps of obsolescent patriarchy—aim to re-mold American society into gender roles that play to and placate weaknesses and deny access to each person's and family's birthright of wholeness. Boyhood Reimagined is both a model and a long-overdue celebration."

— Candace Walsh, co-editor, *Dear John I Love Jane* and *Greetings from Janeland*

"There is no better time for this book. *Boyhood Reimagined* offers a roadmap and reassurance to any parent trying to raise a boy who is 'loving, nurturing, and collaborative.' The essays and interviews in this book give me hope that as a society we can, indeed, raise sons who embody healthy and happy masculinity and become role models for all of us!"

— Kate Hopper, author of *Ready for Air: A Journey Through Premature Motherhood* and *Use Your Words: A Writing Guide for Mothers*

BOYHOOD Reimagined

STORIES OF QUEER MOMS RAISING SONS

Edited by Ada Malone
and Gail Marlene Schwartz

Text copyright © 2025 by Ada Malone and Gail Marlene Schwartz
All rights reserved. Printed in the United States of America
Published by Motina Books, LLC, Highlands Ranch, CO
www.MotinaBooks.com

Library of Congress Cataloguing-in-Publication Data
Names: Malone, Ada and Schwartz, Gail Marlene
Title: Boyhood Reimagined/Malone and Schwartz
Description: First Edition. | Highlands Ranch:
Motina Books, 2025

Identifiers:
LCCN: 2025932935

ISBN-13: 979-8-88784-057-4 (hardcover)
ISBN-13: 979-8-88784-050-5 (ebook)
ISBN-13: 979-8-88784-049-9 (paperback)

Subjects:
FAMILY & RELATIONSHIPS / LGBTQ+
FAMILY & RELATIONSHIPS / Parenting / Motherhood
SOCIAL SCIENCE / LGBTQ+ Studies / General

Cover Design: Erin Needham
Illustrations: Erin Needham

Dedication

For Erin, Lucie, and Alexi, my co-conspirators in
reimagining boyhood.
~GMS

For Levi—the boy who changed it all—and for Dawn
who works tirelessly for our little family.
~AMM

"I heard a saying a long time ago that we love our sons and raise our daughters.
What if we did both, with all genders?"

~Sonora Jha, *How to Raise a Feminist Son*

Table of Contents

FOREWORD I

INTRODUCTION..9

Ada.. 9

Gail.. 11

Some Background Research 12

Our Contribution to the Conversation........................... 20

Who are "Queer Moms"?....................................... 24

DYKES RAISING SONS   by June BlueSpruce 29

MAKING INVISIBLE WORK VISIBLE TO RAISE

HEALTHY MEN   by Katherine Mack 37

GOD'S WORK: INTERVIEW WITH THE RAPICAVOLI-

GONZALES FAMILY   by Jolivette Mecenas 43

WHERE ARE THE PRINCESS SHIRTS FOR BOYS?   by

Irina González 55

THE ULTIMATE ACT OF DEFIANCE   by Robin Lowey

.... 63

INTERVIEW: SABRINA WHITE   by Gail Marlene

Schwartz 73

A SET OF TOO-PRETTY SHEETS   by Devon Ward85

INTERVIEW: BROOKE STRAUSS   by Ada Malone91

MARRIAGE AND FAMILY   by Amy Hinze-Pifer..101

WALKING WHILE FEMALE: WHAT I WANT MY SON

TO KNOW   by Marie Holmes 107

INTERVIEW: ELLIOTT O. WRIGHT AND KATE OKESON

by Ada Malone 113

THE SALAD SPINNER CHRONICLES   by Gail Marlene

Schwartz 121

ONE FAMILY'S JOURNEY EXPLORING EMOTIONAL

SENSITIVITY   by Brie Radis.............................129

GINGERBREAD PERSONS AND STAYING OUT OF OUR KIDS' WAY: INTERVIEW WITH MEADOW AND JENN BRAUN by Ada Malone 135

TIME TO CHANGE THE CHANNEL   by Lalita du Perron 145

SOAPBOX   by Ada Malone............................ 151

INTERVIEW: ANGIE RUNDLE   by Gail Marlene Schwartz 159

GUY TIME   by Gail Marlene Schwartz............. 167

A PUNK PLAYLIST FOR QUEER MOMS RAISING FEMINIST BOYS   By Jolivette Mecenas 175

ABOUT THE CONTRIBUTORS.......................... 184

ACKNOWLEDGEMENTS 205

BIBLIOGRAPHY 207

FOREWORD

In 1990s San Francisco, my mothers joined a small but mighty group of queer women making history by embarking on the journey of motherhood. Nearly three decades later, as I write this foreword for a book highlighting the experiences of many lesbian mothers raising boys, I recognize that my upbringing was a gift, maybe even my superpower.

From the moment I became conscious of myself and the world around me, I was aware that I had two loving mothers and a cool older brother. Nothing about my conception was ever a mystery to me—my parents were lesbians, and my biological father was a sperm donor who I would never have a relationship with. One of my moms gave birth to me, and the other gave birth to my brother. When I turned 18 years old, I learned more details: The sperm donor who made my birth possible also donated to other queer moms, leading to the birth of a dozen half siblings who share my DNA and a similar backstory. But that is a tale for another day.

When my brother and I were very young, my moms explained to us that our nontraditional family was not at all a source of shame, but rather of absolute pride. We learned that diversity is inherent to our humanity and that our differences give us strength. They made sure we understood this firsthand by witnessing the power and beauty of the gay community. Every year we would spend "Gay Day," one of the largest and most spirited Pride celebrations in the world, marching in the streets of San Francisco. We were two little boys growing up in the queer capital of the world, surrounded by highly educated, successful lesbians and gay men, including queer icons Harvey Milk and Billie Jean King serving as our personal heroes. In 2004, then–San Francisco Mayor Gavin Newsom facilitated the first ever same-sex marriages in the United States, and my moms—who had already been together for over 20 years at the time—were one of the lucky couples to tie the knot. Those experiences shaped our identities for life.

At the same time, we were aware of the hatred and intolerance directed toward our community. Shortly after my parents got married, same-sex marriage was once again banned, and their marriage license was voided by the California Supreme Court. In 2008, Proposition 8, a constitutional amendment intended to ban same-sex marriage for good, passed in California. I distinctly re-member being 12 years old, feeling so positive about the outcome of the upcoming vote while marching against Prop 8 in downtown San Francisco, only to be crushed when it passed days later. A close friend of mine revealed that his father—a mentor to me and a local sports legend—voted yes on Prop 8. Even though he respected me and my family, he was religious and wanted to protect the "sanctity of marriage" by reserving it exclusively for heterosexual couples.

Even in our liberal Northern California bubble, the concept of openly gay women having children—two boys no less—was unheard of by many of my peers and their parents. I was used to being peppered with questions from my friends:

"Which one is your real mom?"

"They both are," I would answer matter-of-factly.

"Don't you wish you had a dad?"

"Not really—my moms are frickin' awesome."

This second question, with its implied disapproval, opened my eyes to the prevalence of androcentrism and heteronormativity. What could these fathers offer that my mothers could not? One of my moms coached my Little League team and never missed the opportunity to take me surfing or join me in the backyard to shoot hoops. My other mom took me to MLB games, taught me how to drive a stick shift, and gave me the birds-and-the-bees talk when the time was right. Our household was so safe, happy, and full of love. I didn't feel like I was missing out whatsoever—this whole "dad" thing seemed hugely overrated.

Anecdotally, many of my friends' fathers didn't connect deeply with their sons, instead putting pressure on them to act more macho, avoid "girly" things, and prioritize sports or other interests that they deemed manly. The fathers who *were* kind and supportive were more than happy to spend time with me and answer any male-specific questions I might have. In my eyes, I had the best possible arrangement: two engaged, loving parents who happened to be badass feminist trailblazers focused on making the world a more equitable place.

Through it all, I had a wonderful and privileged childhood. On the surface, I was just another white, heterosexual, cisgender male from an affluent Bay Area community. Beyond the aforementioned microaggressions, I mostly avoided direct discrimination and was never forced to question my identity or change how I presented myself in order to feel safe. But on the inside, I felt different. I was part of the queer community and wasn't afraid to say it! For me and my older brother, Max, "Queer Spawn" was the rallying cry, and the school grounds were our battlefield. When homophobic epithets were hurled toward vulnerable youth in our community, Max and I stood up to the bullies, even if we weren't the ones taking the brunt of it.

In 2001, our family moved from San Francisco across the Golden Gate Bridge to the suburbs of Marin County, an area that was much more strongly oriented toward homogeneity and heteronormativity. "When we moved out of the city and into the suburbs, there were a lot fewer queer people in our community, and I felt it right away," Max shared with me in a recent conversation.

> I was in sixth grade, the new kid at school, and basically all the kids were learning swear words for the first time and exploring that. So of course they used homophobic terms. I was this small, new kid who

would speak up and say, "Hey, don't say 'faggot.'" And I got bullied—nothing hardcore, but I would get told to shut up or take a solid punch to the arm. But that didn't stop me from standing up to them. By eighth grade, I had grown about 10 inches. At that point, when I said, "Don't say 'faggot,'" they listened.

Max was able to use his confidence, perseverance, and later his physical stature to command respect and begin a cultural shift. By the time he was a senior in high school, he had an entire army of queer friends and straight allies who upheld a firm "no homophobia tolerated" culture throughout the school, helping create a safer and more comfortable environment for queer or questioning kids in our community. As his younger brother, I was left with a clear roadmap, and big shoes to fill.

I accepted the challenge. In middle school and high school, I focused on upholding the standard my brother set. In college, my friends and I made it clear that our apartment was a "no homophobia tolerated" zone, an idea taken directly from Max's success in high school. However, it was harder to calmly educate drunken fraternity bros than I anticipated, and simple requests to avoid gay slurs or treat my queer friends with respect turned ugly on more than one occasion. Once, I recruited my enormous friends on the rugby team to help keep the peace during a confrontation that occurred after I told a random partygoer to check his language in our home. On his way out, the guy smashed the windshield of my roommate's car.

From middle school to high school, at university, and

into my adult life, I have always proudly identified as a feminist and a member of the queer community in my own way—an "inside man" existing in a world still largely controlled by straight white males. These days, I work in international development and live in Rwanda, East Africa, where I continue to push the envelope, engaging with the increasingly visible queer and feminist communities here and advocating for their safety and rights to the best of my ability. My privilege allows me to blend into straight, male-dominated spaces and vocally advocate for LGBTQIA+ and gender rights, while coming from a uniquely informed background. My unusual upbringing has given me a purpose, my very own superpower with which to view and impact the world.

But beyond the personal significance of my experiences lies a broader societal importance. The stories and perspectives in this book have so much value to the world—not only to other queer families dealing with similar issues but also to the broader public, who may still be wrapping their heads around the idea of queer women raising boys. For example, Brie Radis's wonderful essay highlights the statistic that 23% of young men believe that males need to use violence and aggression to earn respect, and Radis states that one of her goals as a mother is to ensure that her 11-year-old son doesn't fall into that group. In my own life, a hallmark of my two-mother, no-father childhood was nonviolence, framed by a belief that as a society we have evolved past the need for men to demonstrate physical aggression to gain respect or social capital.

While my brother and I were taught to stand up and

defend ourselves when necessary, we always focused on using our conviction and intellect to combat ignorance rather than immediately resorting to violence. This was not an easy task—whether it was my brother's growth spurt in middle school allowing his voice to be heard or my rugby friends' strength that protected my home in college, physicality was absolutely equated with masculinity and respect throughout my adolescence. I believe my mothers' feminist teachings played a critical role in helping us understand these dynamics and develop strategies to gain others' respect without displaying violent or aggressive behavior.

Radis's parenting goal, in connection with my own lived experience, illustrates one of my core takeaways from this book, which I hope will be gleaned by all who read it: Deglamorizing toxic masculinity and violence in the lives of young boys leads to less trauma and healthier adolescent development, which in turn creates a positive feedback loop of healthy masculinity, benefiting the safety and well-being of all young people.

Ideas such as this are what makes this book so important. By highlighting the experiences and ambitions of lesbian mothers raising sons, it challenges conventional notions of masculinity, family, and parenthood and offers a glimpse into the lives of families like mine that defy stereotypes and break barriers. By sharing our stories, it challenges the status quo and paves the way for a more inclusive future.

As I look back on my own journey, I am filled with gratitude for the trailblazing women who showed me the way. I thank my moms, and all the queer moms out there, for taking on the patriarchy with remarkable courage and influencing lasting change within mainstream society. Your legacy will live on in the pages of this book and in the hearts of the children you raised. Thank you for gifting us our very own superpowers.

So let us celebrate our differences, embrace our uniqueness, teach our children about concepts such as feminism and intersectionality, and continue to fight for a world where every family is celebrated regardless of its composition. For as I have learned, it is our differences that give us strength and our love that binds us together.

Sam Waterstone
Writer, Consultant, and Queerspawn

INTRODUCTION

Ada

I never planned to become a mom, much less a #boymom. I never could have anticipated one day cringing at the problematic stereotypes and gender constructs underlying that hashtag while simultaneously feeling myself nodding in recognition at the social media posts describing all the farting, fighting, messes, and near-death stunts associated with being a #boymom. When my posse of lesbian comrades started to have babies in their mid- to late 30s, I began noticing how many of them had one or more boys. For so long we had lived in a women-centered world that wasn't at all, of course, representative of the larger world. We lived by our own rules, breaking from societal expectations, bonding with and understanding one another as queer women. Suddenly we were supposed to know what to do with these humans— these future men—smack dab in the center of our lives.

During every annual check-up for the first five years of my son's life, my wife and I would nervously ask our male pediatrician, "Is his penis okay?" "Should it look like that?" and "Is the pee coming out normally?" and plead, "Please help us with this appendage we know nothing about!"

While I don't know much about penises, I do know a fair amount about gender. I know about men and how I've been treated by some of them. I know about the harm some of them have caused by helping shape a world where violence and sexual assault of women can be brushed off as "locker room talk." But I also know and love a lot of wonderful men, and I know that they, too, have lived under the influence of a patriarchal society. Those feminist men among us have had to overcome a lot to treat women the way they do and reside in their own masculinity, which might appear different from that of the men around them. I also know that gender is a construct, a continuum—that it is fluid. I know this as a queer woman who came out as femme but then decided to present as more masculine and now, years later, feels most comfortable somewhere in between; I am finally willing to admit that I like dresses and was once a cheerleader. I began to imagine what my lesbian friends raising boys might learn from one another and what the world of parenting might learn from us if we wrote about our experiences. And so, I called on my longtime dear friend Gail, another writer and queer mom raising a son.

Gail

I REMEMBER THAT moment the ultrasound tech told my wife and I we were having a boy. I cried. My own fantasy for parenthood had always involved a daughter. What was I going to do with a son? How was I going to continue my activism and feminism while pouring all my energy into another white male? And what if, God forbid, I just couldn't love him fully?

Fast forward 14 years, and the questions seem absurd. My son and I are incredibly close, and my parenting has actually grown around my activism. In a way, I've come to see that the work done with boys has a critical impact on shaping a more egalitarian world. My early sense of loss morphed into an understanding that I couldn't have healed generational trauma with a daughter like I've been able to with my son. And generational trauma is such a key piece of breaking down patriarchy and other systems of oppression.

But what hasn't become crystal clear yet is how my son's parenting, now by two moms and a nonbinary stepparent, is impacting his own identity. I hated that his attention was captivated by cement mixers, 18-wheelers, and now Minecraft. I hated that the feminist parenting Lucie and I have given him since day one has seemed to not have any impact on his growling and tackling us or his desire to win at every single game *every. single. time.* My dad often told a cautionary tale about a homeschooled boy in a remote village. His parents were peace activists, and they never uttered the word "gun," let alone exposed their son to weapons. One day, the boy pointed a tuna sandwich at his mom and said, "Bang bang." I hated the idea that my dad might be right, but I wondered.

Some Background Research

WE BEGAN WITH SOME questions we wanted to explore: How does being parented by queer moms impact a boy's gender development and overall understanding of gender? Can women who love women raise boys with a healthy relationship to gender and masculinity? Do queer moms who practice feminist parenting raise feminist boys? What do straight feminist parents have to learn from us?

Although these questions aren't new, they are certainly contemporary ones, ones that in many countries, including the US, have been evolving with the passage of LGBTQIA+ laws, including marriage and adoption rights for non-biological parents. And even though these laws exist, we Americans understand deeply, especially with the recent reversal of *Roe v. Wade,* that they may not be ones we can count on for the long term. The question, then, becomes even more important, as 2017 census data showed there were between 2 and 3.7 million children under the age of 18 being raised by an LGBTQIA+ parent (Day 2017).

To address these questions, we needed to dig up some history from a time when lesbian and single moms were often believed to be incapable of raising boys adequately without a father or male role model in the home. In her book *We Are Family*, researcher Susan Golombok explains that in the 1970s, early on in the gay rights movement, lesbian moms who had been in heterosexual marriages were never awarded custody precisely because of their orientation (Golombok 2020, 16). The reasoning behind these decisions, which would be shocking today, was threefold: (1) Lesbian moms were considered incapable of good parenting, (2) The children would suffer long-term psychological harm from being picked on at school and, most relevantly, for this collection, and (3) Girls and boys would lack appropriate gender identity. At that time, no researcher had undertaken the subject, so prevailing norms guided legal decisions, with heartbreaking results. As lesbian women came out and it became more common for queer women to fight for custody, those norms were exposed; not only were lesbians systematically denied custody but oftentimes judges would write in their orders that during visits a queer mom was not allowed to sleep in the same bedroom as her partner (17).

As a young researcher, Golombok embraced the scientific challenge of studying the well-being of children parented by lesbian women, and in 1977 she became a pioneer in her field. She and her colleagues carefully designed intricate studies to measure lesbian mothers' capacity and the children's psychological health and gender identities. Years of research overwhelmingly showed that compared with children of traditional parents, children of lesbian moms had warm and involved parenting, their psychological health was as strong, and their gender identities were proportionately similar (Golombok 2020, 21). Two American researchers in the field, Martha Kirkpatrick at the University of California Los Angeles and Richard Green at State University of New York at Stony Brook, came to similar conclusions with similar studies.

Later, in the 1980s, American Dr. Nanette Gartrell initiated longitudinal studies of lesbian parents who became parents via donor insemination. Once again, the news was good.

Their findings revealed that "... adolescents raised in lesbian families demonstrated higher levels of social, school/academic, and total competence than teenagers from traditional heterosexual families. Furthermore, adolescents in this study experienced lower levels of social problems, rule-breaking, aggressive, and externalizing problem behavior than their age-matched counterparts" (Gartrell and Bos 2010). What was interesting to us was not that the children of lesbian parents were okay, although this certainly was and is politically and socially critical for the viability of our families. What was interesting to us was that the children studied actually appeared to be faring *better* in certain ways than children from traditional families. Lower rates of aggression, rule-breaking, and acting out sounded to us like the possible emergence of healthy masculinity.

Obviously, we were not the only ones interested in these findings. When Dr. Peggy Drexler studied lesbian families and single moms in the mid-'90s for her 2005 book *Raising Boys Without Men: How Maverick Moms are Creating the Next Generation of Exceptional Men*, her work on boys' development was considered groundbreaking. Even after 20 years, lesbian families at that time were flying under the cultural radar. And households without men frequently bore public scrutiny, with the question about effectiveness of parenting without dads posed repeatedly despite the findings of Golombok, Gartrell, and many other researchers. Drexler's book responded to that scrutiny, proving that with thorough, systemic research, parenting without dads does not lead to any kind of failure—behavioral, intellectual, or otherwise—for sons. In fact, building on Gartrell's findings, Drexler discovered that "lesbian mothers scored higher on the moral attitude scale than their heterosexual counterparts and were more likely to create opportunities for their sons to examine moral and values issues. They were also more likely to talk about morality in terms of broader social implications" (Drexler 2007, 19).

It is now almost two decades since Golombok, Gartrell, and Drexler began their groundbreaking work. Since Drexler's book was published, lesbian families have become more commonplace, and queer parenting has gained more acceptance over the years, especially for white, middle-class, cisgender families. This acceptance, however, despite readily available research backing it up, is still absolutely dependent on who and where you are. While schools in Florida are outlawing any mention of queerness, schools in New York are celebrating diversity during Pride month.

All this still stands in contrast to the years (and years prior) in which those researchers did their work, a time when there was a more general public sentiment that queer families—especially families without men—were somehow lacking and detrimental to effective child-rearing. The combination of broader acceptance and the challenge this acceptance has precipitated creates a unique historic moment. It is in this moment that our collection revisits queer moms raising sons to explore how these families that lack consistent, direct male influence navigate gender in general, masculinity in particular, and how those choices impact the boys.

Progressive thinking in this contemporary moment has evolved since Drexler wrote, so we quickly found out that our territory needed a different approach. Intersectionality is now a commonplace concept in leftist circles, and activists and intellectuals understand the ways race, gender, sexuality, and even class are all tools of patriarchy and capitalism. Manifesting intersectionality was a struggle for us. We made many efforts of targeted outreach to queer parents of color, but unfortunately, the white contributors in the collection far outweigh the BIPOC contributors. Obviously, having two white women as editors is part of the issue, and yet the idea for the book was born in the context of our friendship. This is one area that felt unresolved.

Another challenge was integrating intersectionality into how we talked about the issues. We collectively want to promote a new version of the world beyond patriarchy, one we are parenting our sons for, yet we also acknowledge that this new world hasn't been created yet. One particular example was whether to capitalize the "w" in white. Many social justice-oriented sources along with reputable mainstream organizations are now using an upper-case "w"; the public conversation has become quite nuanced. The two of us and our publisher felt strongly that capitalizing "w" implied white supremacy, so we chose to leave it lower-case. This experience pointed out the murkiness of the path leading to our goals. How on earth can we change boyhood profoundly enough to give birth to this world when we don't feel able to discuss the issues inclusively yet? Remaining curious, we continued our research.

In her book *How to Raise a Feminist Son*, Sonora Jha describes how "boyhood, especially in America, has become some sort of battleground" (Jha 2021, 3). That "battleground" was described by Donald Trump in 2018 when he declared, "It is a very scary time for young men in America, where you can be guilty of something you may not be guilty of" (Diamond 2018). This statement was made in response to the allegations against Supreme Court Justice Brett Kavanaugh (a then-nominee for the Supreme Court) by Christine Blasey Ford. More broadly, Trump's proclamation was a response to the #MeToo movement that had gained momentum the year prior. Those of us who had donned pussy hats and brought our sons to women's marches the year before continued to be outraged that this kind of toxic masculinity could not only continue to exist but be elected to office and rule our country. This collection was born out of these moments, which reminded us that feminism continues to be critically needed and that we still have a long way to go in terms of achieving gender equity and freedom from "rape culture." How do we raise boys to ensure this does not happen again?

The contributors are a group of feminist thinkers, writers, and queer moms who came together to collectively think through these questions via writing about their experiences. Through these essays, stories, and interviews, we hope to show that in the years since researchers proved that being a single- or two-mom household does not harm children, queer moms have managed to do something more than simply stake out a space for ourselves as parents. Now that we are not under constant critique, we ask, Can we turn our energies toward raising boys with healthy parenting choices that provide an antidote to the troubling patriarchal culture that continues to dominate despite numerous waves of feminist movements?

We turned to Jha's book for answers. She explores her life as a single Indian mother with a disability trying to raise a son in the US. A "village" of feminist women, both single and coupled, from various cultures helped Jha raise her son after a life-threatening car crash left her unable to function on her own. She became concerned that perhaps this village was going "too far" and asked, "Would the marked absence of men in my village harm my boy?" (Jha 2021). It turns out that her answer was no, and this collection is here to further illustrate that.

Likewise, Drexler's overall message was that "parenting is not anchored to gender" (Drexler 2007, xiv), and she describes the lesbian-led households she researched as having "non-gender-based parenting" (204). And while we are supportive of this concept as a way forward for all parents, we are also interested in looking at the ways in which households without men can possibly provide a unique space within which to raise a new generation of boys that are active co-conspirators in the dismantling of patriarchy. Through the families included here, we are looking closely at how careful attention to gender and feminism within queer households might help shape a future population of antiracist and nonmiso-gynistic men. We're curious about how queer moms are consciously thinking of different, perhaps more radical ways to parent boys in a culture that continues to reify stereotypical versions of masculinity and perpetuate things such as harassment and sexual assault.

Along these same lines, Drexler (2007) writes, "The reality is that it's how a family acts, not the way it's made up, that determines whether the children succeed or fail" (10). And in part, that is what this collection is about: how queer moms act in the face of raising boys in a patriarchal culture and how we confront gender stereotypes and break gender constructs in the name of raising boys with healthier notions about gender and masculinity than previous generations.

In her book, Jha explains that toxic masculinity is "a cultural concept of manliness that glorifies stoicism, strength, virility, dominance, and violence, and that is socially maladaptive or harmful to boys' own mental health" (Jha 2021, 8). She also maintains that people of any gender can "build a gentle and vital masculinity from the ground up" (9). And we agree with her; we hope people of all genders along the spectrum collectively work to build families free from gender stereotypes. However, as queer women, we have spent years acutely aware of our gender and the violence lodged against it.

We are not here to say that queer moms are "better" moms than heterosexual, feminist moms. Likewise, we are not here to say that fathering, whether done by straight or gay/queer men, cannot be done in a feminist manner. The fact is that marginalized people who have historically faced discrimination often have a raised consciousness—especially about matters that affect them directly but also about the plight of others who face similar outsider experiences. As such, queer moms hold a unique position of having often faced intersectional discrimination on account of both their gender and their sexual orientation. Queer moms are frequently feminist and often have a heightened awareness of gender issues. We cannot assume, of course, that all queer moms identify as feminist, but those of us who have contributed to and/or have been interviewed for this collection do. Several contributors share their own journeys to becoming feminists at the end of this book with their bios.

Our Contribution to the Conversation

THIS COLLECTION CONTAINS both essays by and interviews with queer moms raising sons with the goal of creating a better world. With odds seemingly stacked against us as we look at the results of the 2024 election, with Republicans holding power in all three chambers of government and a majority on the Supreme Court, we are likely to see radical shifts to the right, including bans on same-sex marriage and outlaws on discussing race in schools. As we head into an uncertain future with a second Trump administration, it's more important than ever to capture how queer moms are thinking about the intersection of their parenting choices and the development of healthy masculinity.

Many of the anecdotes contained in this collection do not have concrete answers for how to raise sons who can begin to change the patriarchal culture we live in. Like most parents of all identities, many of the writers and interviewees are deep in the thick mess that is parenting—trying to figure things out as we go and consistently being surprised by what our kids bring back to us. We are all aware of what we are up against: social and peer pressures outside the home that might look very different from the kind of gender-aware philosophies that undergird our parenting. We are all simply trying our best. Yet you will see that these writers and interviewees hold a keen awareness of the ways in which a mom-only household by default models femininity as a norm and female strength as a given. As Jha puts it, "When we surround a child with the people and values we consider important, they seek out more of the same" (Jha 2021, 74).

Contributors are also devoted to increasing their sons' intersectional sensitivities. As members of the queer community and allies of trans and nonbinary folx, some who play a role in this collection, there is also a lot of discussion around teaching our sons about gender fluidity and gender norms as a construct. There are sons in this collection wearing dresses one day and baseball caps the next. There are sons reminding the moms of their own lessons about gender norms and stereotypes. And there are sons happily doing domestic duties as well as those resisting it.

The essays in this collection also discuss the ways in

which issues of race collide with and impact sexism and the kinds of parenting choices queer moms make. There are candid, honest portrayals of moms frozen with fear upon learning that the biological sex of their unborn child was male. There is also the recognition, upon having a son, that while the children's book market currently has a lot of female empowerment books, there is a dearth of books modeling boys as thoughtful, careful, feminist humans. In this collection, however, there are frank discussions about the ways in which some stereotypical male behavior is now a part of our lives through the actions of our sons. In particular, moms in *Boyhood Reimagined* acknowledge their sons' needs for a kind of aggressive physicality that isn't typically seen in young girls. Some of the sons described in this collection *need* to wrestle; they need to work out their energy through the use of their bodies in relationship to the bodies of others. How to handle this in ways that are safe and establish boundaries is a challenge and a focus in mothering sons. These kinds of body-centered interactions are also closely tied to the concept of consent, something many parents these days are concerned with.

Additionally, this collection illustrates some moms using popular music to teach the differences between punishment and consequences while trying to raise a child who learns from the latter more than he experiences the former. And there are also moms who use punk music to connect with their children in a shared feminist ideology. While music and art are wonderful for storytelling and can be great teachers, they are also vehicles that carry mainstream values and ideas into our sons' lives. In *How to Raise a Feminist Son*, Jha describes the importance of editing and curating our sons' libraries while we still have the power to do so and then, when they are older, helping them contextualize the stories they read through conversation. She recommends asking them questions such as, "Who needs help or rescue, and who is doing the helping or rescuing? Who is working hard to prove they are worthy, and who is seen as worthy from the start?" (Jha 2021, 57). One of the interviews contained in this collection addresses these questions by discussing the male-centric pronoun usage found in so many children's books. Some moms describe altering the wording of these books in order to decenter "he" as default for all the trucks, animals, and toys. The world centers our boys already. As Jha puts it, "We must tell the story, tweak it, nudge our kids toward curiosity, poke fun at some tropes, question stereotypes, and course correct as our kids push back or feel left behind … What this all means is that we ourselves commit to renewed joy of reading and also reading between the lines" (52).

These stories have one significant experience in common: the societal forces pushing in on our parenting approaches and families. While all the families featured in this collection model female empowerment and teach consent, gender fluidity, and kindness, each day we continue to face sons who come home having been shaped by a society that still devalues motherhood and women and teaches violence and the gender binary as normal—especially for boys.

Who are "Queer Moms"?

WHEN WE FIRST BEGAN WORK on this collection, the concept seemed simple: women writing about their experiences loving women who parented boys. But once we posted our call for submissions, we started getting questions from writers, and it soon became obvious that the categories of moms and sons are murky, fluid, and understood differently by different people. Are trans women moms? Would we accept a piece from masculine-presenting nonbinary parents assigned female at birth? What about a bisexual woman raising a child with a trans man? How about butch lesbians who don't identify as mothers? Who is identifying sons as such, the children themselves or their moms? We found ourselves often grappling with language and in ways that were very different from the turn-of-the-century when researchers like Drexler were writing on this topic. Words such as "mom," "woman," "feminist," "queer," "boy," and "son" are all now problematic in thorny ways that people were not as aware of then.

After much consideration, we chose to use the term "queer" as something of a shorthand for those whose sexualities or gender identities exist outside the mainstream, as illustrated in many aspects of our stories. Though we ended up using the term "queer moms" and welcoming all who identified with the term to contribute, we simultaneously understand the problematic nature of this, as patriarchal culture is the context in which this book, like our lives, exists. But when we think about gender as a construct, it follows that we can then undo or deconstruct it. For some in the queer community, this means toppling concepts of gender until they are nonexistent, and we all live along some kind of fluid gender spectrum.

We also needed to grapple with what we meant when we called for households that excluded a consistent male presence. Throughout this collection, you will see that most of the families address with their children—their sons in particular—the idea of gender as constructed and gender stereotypes as meaningless, yet the contributors and interviewees clearly identify as female/mom and have children who were assigned male at birth and identify as boys. While we seek to complicate ideas around gender, we also still see gender as a "thing." Ocean Vuong describes this idea beautifully when he discusses what masculinity means to him in an interview with Glennon Doyle: "I don't think the work is finished in maleness. Just because it's been poorly demonstrated does not mean that it's finished, that it's exhausted. It might just be beginning. And because it's also a destination for so many. Masculinity as an expression is a destination for so many trans folks. So, I don't want to leave it behind because I'm also concerned that those who are in charge of it or have been in power of it would sort of ruin it further" (Doyle 2022). The ethos of this collection echoes Vuong's belief that just because maleness has been "poorly demonstrated" does not mean it is finished. How we help shape it for the future is at the heart of this book.

Additionally, we honor the idea of a particular gender as a "destination" for trans folx by welcoming all women/moms and all male/sons to participate. This means that nonbinary individuals who don't identify as a mother or a son aren't included here. This is not to say that they don't have important or interesting parenting stories of their own but that their stories are simply beyond the purview of this collection. Here we are exploring gender specifically constructed, and in particular we are interested in households in which the gender of the parents is marginalized (female) and the gender of the sons is privileged (male). Like Vuong, then, we "don't want to throw language away, [we] don't want to throw all the gender expressions away because there's still something of value, of use" (Doyle 2022).

In the end, we left it up to individual writers and interviewees to decide how they identify, and we made it as simple as we could: If you identify as both queer and a mom and you have a son, then we want to include your story.

DYKES RAISING SONS
by June BlueSpruce

"Ooh, you *girl!*" says one nine-year-old boy taunting another in the next room.

"Shhhh! My mom can hear you," urges our younger son. He knows what's coming.

I stand in the doorway, leaning on the jamb. The boys stop their play. One looks at me, curious as to how I will respond; another avoids my gaze. Our son tenses.

"Calling someone a girl is not an insult in this house," I say in a matter-of-fact tone. It's what I say every time. I leave them to their play, quieter now.

"I *told* you!" our son hisses.

My partner Martha and I birthed two sons at a time when it was a radical act for a lesbian to get pregnant. Our older son dove in first, in January 1980, conceived by Martha using donor sperm and born at home on Capitol Hill in Seattle. Our second son came through me in

November 1983, conceived using a different donor and born at a different home but with the same otherworldly, miraculous energy. Life longs for life. Our home was full of it, bursting the seams of our bodies and lives, turning them inside out and upside down.

Our lives as young, middle-class white women from mainstream Republican families had already been upended by the civil rights and anti-war movements, second-wave feminism, and queer liberation. We had moved far away from our families—from Tulsa, Oklahoma, and Swarthmore, Pennsylvania—to come out in the early 1970s. As young dykes, we asserted our right and ability to be independent from men. This was a renegade idea, as until 1974, banks could refuse a woman credit without her husband's signature. We lived in collective households with other lesbian feminists, rejecting heteronormative relationships and individualistic ways of thinking and acting and trying to deconstruct sexism, homophobia, racism, classism, and capitalism.

At that time, many women, lesbian and heterosexual alike, experienced and expressed anger at men in general. Sexism and homophobia ran rampant; in many states, marital rape was still legal and anti-sodomy laws were enforced. Women I knew had been ignored, silenced, mistreated, denied jobs, harassed, molested, raped by men. I was angry at ex-boyfriends who had mistreated me, random men on the street who yelled catcalls or exposed themselves, and male employers who harassed and propositioned me. Angry because I had been taught all my life to hide my intelligence, my body, my periods, my sexuality. Our collective rage had a sharp edge, like new scissors cutting through outgrown clothing.

Both Martha and I had men in our lives whom we loved. We believed that men were not doomed to be oppressive; they were taught to be. Now we were the teachers. After our sons were born, we wrestled with the question, How could we love them for exactly who they were, all of who they were, and raise them in a culture that disrespected and devalued who we were? How could we let them go to find their own paths, to challenge or conform to that culture?

Our first answer was to love ourselves and them, to model kind love, fierce love, love that allowed for mistakes—including our own, which were many. We needed to manage our own stories and feelings—rage, pain, fear, despair—so that our sons wouldn't bear that burden. This is much easier to write than it was to do. Martha and I both grew up in families where feelings, if expressed at all, came out indirectly. We had different responses. I tended to head right into intense emotions, including conflict; having everything out in the open felt better to me than suppressing it. Martha tended to avoid, deflect, distract. Years of therapy, individually and as a couple, helped me step back and Martha step forward. Our sons also differed sharply in the ways they processed feelings. The older one was more kinesthetic, the younger one more verbal. House meetings to talk things out didn't always work; we tried to model behavior in simple, clear ways.

Our second answer was to tell them the truth about the world: the ways people collaborate with and nurture one another and the ways people hurt, stereotype, and dominate. Tell them in age-appropriate terms, when they were ready, when they asked us. Tell them when an opportunity came—a book or movie, a playground taunt, a question. There is no better way to clarify and strengthen one's values than to field an unexpected question from a child's inquiring mind. Once, when our older son was very young, a neighbor saw us meandering down the sidewalk and asked me if I was his mother. The neighborhood was new to us and less queer-friendly than Capitol Hill. Not ready to deal with a conversation about our nontraditional family, I said no. Afterward, our son asked me why I responded that way. I had some explaining to do, to him and to myself.

Our lesbian community supported us in a world that wanted us invisible, silenced, gone. Lesbians in the Bay Area showed us how to get pregnant through an informal community network that sidestepped homophobic medical institutions. Seattle friends delivered sperm donations while keeping the donors' and our identities secret. They welcomed our boys, held them, cared for them, cared for us. A small cadre of lesbian moms and their sons held us close.

Most of our lesbian friends, however, didn't have children and couldn't fully understand our experience as parents. So we reached out to gay men and heterosexual parents to fill the gaps. We knew we held a lot of power over how our sons perceived themselves as men. In raising them, we needed to hold a vision of men as loving, nurturing, and collaborative. To hold that vision, we needed relationships with men who embodied it. And our sons did too.

As our boys grew, we realized they needed men in their lives to help show them how to live in their bodies and navigate relationships they had with other males. The men didn't have to be their biological fathers; uncles, stepdads, trusted friends, teachers, and coaches all could have a role. We sought out specific men to spend time with our sons and began to build a community that included them. As gay men in Seattle began to get sick and die from HIV/AIDS, the impetus to connect became more urgent. Bonds between lesbians and gay men that had been frayed by sexism grew stronger.

But our efforts to find gay men who could commit to helping us raise our sons foundered in the epidemic's tidal wave. Our sons kept asking questions about their donors that our straightforward explanations couldn't satisfy. Then, through a unique set of circumstances, we discovered the identities of our donors, first our older son's and then our younger son's. Each time, trust won over fear; we decided to meet them. We were lucky. Both were caring gay men, and our sons had fulfilling and loving relationships with them. They called and related to these men as "Dad," though we were their primary parents. Our younger son's dad once challenged our role after his verbally abusive partner talked to our son in a demeaning way. When we told the dad he could not spend time with our son if his partner was present, he responded with anger. Our older son's dad sat him down and told him, "June and Martha are in charge." We heard no more about it.

We also needed support from institutions, including childcare, schools, youth-focused organizations, and sports programs. In 1984, when our older son was four, he became one of the first children enrolled in Gentle Dragon, an early childhood education center founded as a nonhierarchical worker collective. The center aimed to offer multilingual care that was free of racism, sexism, and homophobia. Staff included people of different races, genders, and sexual orientations, diversity that extended to every classroom. Claude, a gay male teacher in our older son's classroom, the Chameleons, taught the kids a song about unconditional self-acceptance by Jai Michael Josefs that I can still hear our son belting out.

Later, when we encountered homophobia in organizations and institutions, our Gentle Dragon experience helped us confront it with more confidence. Our older son loved hiking, camping, and mountaineering. We withdrew him from his Boy Scout troop because it was too hard for us, especially his dad, to stay in the closet; we were no match for the Boy Scouts' bigotry. The Mountaineers, in contrast, supported his adventures and our family too. Our younger son joined a 4-H club in a neighboring suburb to raise and show bunnies. Though we didn't come out explicitly, the fact that he had two moms became obvious when we camped with him for a week at the King County Fairgrounds. Some of the parents went to the leader and asked that we be kicked out. Her response? "Over my dead body." Allies make a difference.

When our older son was a teenager, he described the mother of one of his friends to Martha: "She's a dyke." "Dyke" is an insider word; in saying it, we reclaim the power of a weapon used to defame us. Hearing the word "dyke" from the lips of a six-foot-tall heterosexual young man startled us, but he had a right. He was an insider in our world. As a child, he had to fend off as much homophobia as we did. He used the word to say, "She's one of us."

Raising sons opened my heart to loving more deeply than I ever had. It forced me to unearth the bones of anger buried long before they were born. It has enabled me to move through the world with empathy, patience, and hope for all of humanity—at least most of the time. And it has been the hardest work I have ever done.

MAKING INVISIBLE WORK VISIBLE TO RAISE HEALTHY MEN
by Katherine Mack

I yelled at my nine-year-old son yesterday. I know this isn't a good parenting practice, but I was exasperated. As I gathered Lego pieces and texted friends about the logistics of our day, which entailed hangouts with different families in addition to errands, he lay reading on the sofa and asked me when I'd be making pancakes.

In many respects, this is a typical parent–child exchange, regardless of gender. Yet it triggered me because I'm a white, able-bodied, middle-class citizen mothering three children, two of whom are white, male-identified boys. I'm also an anti-racist feminist who's committed to raising my children with an awareness of and appreciation for the work of life, work that continues to be done primarily by women, especially women of color, and work that often remains invisible to men, at times by chance but also often by design. I aim to cultivate a healthy masculinity in my sons, one that involves not only appreciating the life work done by others but noticing and doing that work themselves—without reminders and prodding.

Sociologists define "invisible work" as that which is unpaid, unseen, and unappreciated (Daniels 1987). All kinds of bodies perform invisible work. In recent years, however, the term has appeared most frequently in articles about the uneven division of work that sustains family life in middle-class heterosexual households. These articles advise their assumed reader—the disgruntled woman who has taken on the lion's share of fabric-of-life work—to make her invisible work visible. They encourage couples to name and itemize that work and then to apportion to each member of the couple entire areas of responsibility (such as medical care and dinners) rather than assign individual tasks (such as schedule annual check-ups and make dinner tonight). For the most part, these articles don't address how children can and should contribute to household work nor, more importantly, how to raise men who won't need their partners to educate them to do so.

These articles also don't envision a family structure like mine, which gives me a unique ability to raise men who won't require that kind of coaching. I am an elective single mother with a queer and feminist sensibility, one that compels me to question heteronormative conventions and motivates me to raise children who will not reinforce oppressive norms and practices. I don't have a partner to praise, berate, or educate or with whom I can negotiate a more equitable distribution of the work that sustains our family. I can't do it all, nor do I want to outsource all the work I cannot do. I believe that children should take on this work in age-appropriate ways, because doing life work cultivates awareness of both its toll and rewards.

Boys in middle- and upper-class white families stand to benefit the most from my parenting choice. Becoming more aware of the time, effort, and energy that underpins their success might promote in these boys (and the men they become) an understanding of persistent inequities. They would know that talent and hard work are of course essential but also that invisible work enables and facilitates achievement. Anyone is more likely to become "excellent" in sports, academics, or art when they can devote every minute of their waking hours to play, study, and practice. Ignorance about how the work of others (parents, teachers, coaches, caretakers, housecleaner, etc.) fosters and sustains our success creates blind spots about the obstacles those who do this work face. Relatedly, relieving a boy of responsibility for life work also perpetuates the entitled sense that someone else—often the mother or a low-income woman (typically of color)—should and will perform these tasks for him. In this sense, cultivating a cooperative and contributive masculinity in boys not only benefits individual families but also underpins progressive political goals, as these future men's embodied understanding of life work primes them to support programs and policies that aim for more just treatment of the people who most often do it.

What parenting choices support the goal of nurturing this cooperative and contributive masculinity? To start, I attempt to identify life work out loud, especially that which typically remains invisible. For example, I explain to my children that while it might seem I'm just looking at my agenda, I'm in fact thinking through the logistics of our week and thus cannot immediately answer a question. In other words, my brain is occupied with literally "invisible" work that remains so unless and until I name and call attention to it. I also sit down with my children to brainstorm the work that sustains our family: food (shopping, preparing, and clean-up), housework (organizing, cleaning, repairing), and our social life (coordinating, planning, and driving). We talk about what needs to be done, how much time it takes to do, and who can be responsible for doing what.

I acknowledge that this work isn't always fun and that doing it lessens the time we have for other activities, but I always conclude with these questions: Who should do this work that sustains our family? If we don't do it, who will? I explain that each one of us needs to pitch in so that we can do whatever fun family activity we have on the horizon. I tell them I want to avoid becoming a martyr who is simultaneously resentful and concerned that I'm witnessing, perhaps even supporting, the creation of entitled men. I know they don't understand precisely what I mean. At times, they respond by running away as fast as their little legs can carry them. At other times, though, they respond with wide eyes and questions such as, "What is a 'martyr'?" "What does 'entitled' mean?" Then, after I answer those questions of clarification (not knowing how much of what I say has sunk in), they ask, "What can we do to help?"

For now, this feels like a win. In truth, I say the words as much for myself as for them, both to clarify my feelings and to articulate my commitments. As they mature, however, I believe that the concepts will make more sense to them and that they will lead to generative discussions, heightened consciousness, and more enlightened behavior.

To these ends, rather than yelling at my son, I could've made visible the toll of the largely invisible work I was doing. I could've explained that I couldn't simultaneously gather Legos, think through and communicate the logistics of our day, *and* make pancakes. Then I could've asked my son to help me, to shoulder the life work with me. These parenting choices would help make our home both a training ground for and model of a more equitable world, one in which we, my children and I, share the life work that sustains and enriches us.

GOD'S WORK: INTERVIEW WITH THE RAPICAVOLI-GONZALES FAMILY

by Jolivette Mecenas

I started thinking about writing for this collection after spending an afternoon hiking and talking through the redwoods with my son, Max; two good friends of mine, Emmanuelle and Rosanne; and their son, Gael. While Max's other mom was off sipping cold cocktails with her friends, probably in the shade of an outdoor bar patio, begging off hiking in the heat, I had a chance to catch up with friends I've known since our younger days as so-called Mission dykes. We spent much of our 20s and early 30s drinking at the last queer women's bar in San Francisco, the Lexington Club—a.k.a. "the Lex"—and frequenting girl nights at clubs with names such as "Hot Pants" in the South of Market, Mission, and Castro neighborhoods of San Francisco, circa 2000s. We were like the background characters of a Michelle Tea book, riding bicycles and skateboards through the city or stepping off the J Church train right before vomiting from day drinking too much at Zeitgeist, after which we would order al pastor tacos to settle down our stomachs with a nice layer of porky fat to absorb the next drink. It's a marvel that in our 40s we are now in charge of raising small humans to become functional, even happy, adults.

The day of our hike was a scorcher in Oakland, but the redwood and oak canopies kept us cool. The boys, ages nine and seven, ran off ahead, scampering up tree stumps and yelling noisily. Though our kids have been camping and hiking together since they were toddlers, they always need some time to warm up to one another. Gael is the younger of the two and is sweet and gentle, the friendliest cheerleader of anyone he meets. Max has a harder time reading people and can steamroll you with his atonal, dry sarcasm. Both share a love for Pokémon and Lego, as well as boundless energy and a struggle managing turbulent, often explosive "big feelings." And they both have two moms. As we hiked and talked, our conversation turned to the subject of raising boys.

"We're doing God's work here," mused Emmanuelle, a nonreligious person.

"How so?" I asked.

She talked about how she's observed many of her male friends, straight and gay alike, having a hard time dealing with life. I agreed. I mean, life is challenging, and these days can feel like end-times. I get it. But we were surrounded by strong women—older role models, kick-ass peers, young friends—who seemed to be handling the challenges in less lonely, less self-destructive ways than many of our male friends and family members. What was going on here?

I knew what was going on; I teach feminist critical theory to college students, helping them analyze the constraints of traditional gender roles in literature, language, and rhetoric. These discussions often lead to the darker realms of masculinity: domestic violence, assault, harassment, gun violence, sexism, and homophobia.

A week after that hike, I sat at my desk thinking about how parenting is "God's work." In one sense, we often appeal to our better angels (or in my case, therapy) to guide us through the often-triggering challenges of parenting. And in another sense, raising boys to be able to access a full range of emotions comfortably and openly—and to normalize the fact that boys do cry if they want to—may actually improve humanity. I wanted to continue this conversation with Rosanne and Emmanuelle, so we set up a Zoom date. The following are excerpts from our interview, edited for conciseness. Emmanuelle Rapicavoli is an engineer who manages safe drinking water projects with the Environmental Protection Agency, and Rosanne Gonzales works in banking. They live in San Francisco with now nine-year-old Gael. I interviewed them from my home in Los Angeles on April 30, 2022.

Jolivette: What is your idea of healthy masculinity?

Emmanuelle: I wouldn't say my family conformed to the gender norms of masculinity in terms of roles and responsibilities. I had a traditional mom and dad family, so my mom was more the sporty person who did a lot of the hard labor. Even though they embodied the traditional gender roles, where my dad was the breadwinner and my mom took care of us, … there was a lot of fluidity in their relationship [when it came to things like] who was going to fix the washing machine or run five miles with the kids.

My dad was more interested in fashion and looking good … having more attributes that one might assign to women in the family. He was never one who was super into athletics or watching football games. That kind of formed my idea of what masculinity might embody …. What we try to encourage our son to embody is getting to know himself, being comfortable in his own skin, and building his own self-confidence, not at the expense of others or because of his gender or his sex assigned at birth but because of his own unique characteristics and what his interests are … that he's just free to be him and live up to … the things that both interest him and he's good at, but that there isn't this innate linkage between his sex or gender; it's more about him as an individual.

Jolivette: Is there a conversation you've had in which you've talked about how he identifies as a boy or son? Is that a conversation you've had with him?

Rosanne: We have, yeah.

Emmanuelle: Starting from a young age, I would often bring in stories on gender diversity, just picture books about how different folks identify in terms of their gender identity.

Rosanne: A lot of kids at his school came forward and said they were nonbinary, a couple of kids in his class [who were] his friends, and that opened up the conversation for us to talk a little bit more about what gender is, how [he felt] about [him]self, and how [he was] comfortable identifying. We're very open about that and know he could change his thought process or grow into something and decide, *This is not what I thought*. We want it to be open [so] that he has the ability to change the way he feels [and knows] it's okay not to follow everyone else's path. You can be your own person, you have your own emotions, and we'll support you no matter what.

Jolivette: Wow, that's wonderful. What was his response to that?

Emmanuelle [in a kid's voice]: "Okay, sounds good." [Laughter] I think it's been an evolution. At first he was absorbing things, then it evolved into, "Yeah, no, I'm a boy, I'm a boy. Call me a boy." We're currently at, "I'm comfortable identifying as a boy." Like Rosanne said, the door is always open; if he changes [his mind] or feels differently, we kind of check in periodically just to make sure—

Rosanne: that we're using the appropriate terms or supporting his emotions.

Emmanuelle: Things haven't shifted. [Laughs]

Jolivette: We have similar conversations with our son, but it's definitely been a road for me to get to that place and definitely different from how I grew up. Rosanne, what has been the road for you to get to the place where you can leave the door open for Gael to think about his gender identity?

Rosanne: I grew up with a mom and dad and then with [just] a mom for a while. I had a lot of brothers and sisters. In growing up, there were a lot of rules. The boys were allowed to do certain things, and the girls were not allowed. Growing up, I learned that there were certain sports that girls couldn't play with my brothers and his friends, and my sisters all wanted to play with dolls, and I was like, *yuck*. And so I learned these were the roles, but I didn't like them. And I didn't agree with them because I didn't want to be put in that box. Growing up with that, I didn't want to put Gael in that box. I want him to make the choice and do what interests him. I would've been happier playing [sports] with the boys' than playing with the girls, for my own personality. It has to do with what you like, and not necessarily your gender. I don't agree with it. I don't want to push that on him, how I grew up, especially since I didn't agree with it.

Emmanuelle: Humans, but particularly male-identified humans, in their development need that physical roughhousing and interplay. It's part of establishing boundaries and learning how to interact physically. They need that physical roughhousing but also tender moments. That's an important part of our connection and relation to him, ensuring he's able to get out his physical energy and work through that with us in a safe environment, but we're communicating and establishing.

Rosanne: Boundaries!

Emmanuelle: Appropriate boundaries and testing those out in a safer environment, coupled with his big feelings. Sometimes they're connected to his big feelings, but sometimes … it's just energy!

Rosanne: Sometimes his feelings are connected to something unrelated to what he's actually expressing, and until you get down and talk with him and play with him, he may not express the real cause of his upset until he has some down time.

Jolivette: Hmmm. Rosanne, that's interesting. Do you have an example or story of when that happened?

Rosanne: One time he came home from school, and he was in such a bad mood, like really bad. And angry, upset. He was saying how someone bumped into him at school and didn't say sorry, and he felt hurt. We were talking it through, and it turned out that was not what caused [his bad mood]. It was someone bullying him on the bus. Someone was messing with him on the bus, and that really upset him. [The cause of big feelings] is not always what he says it is. For us it's about finding out what's going on [and asking], "How can we help you? Can we listen to you?"

Emmanuelle: The first step is naming the feeling,

what's going on. That helps him build his own resilience, to be able to name the feeling and then work through it.

Jolivette: I feel like I didn't learn that until my thirties. [Laughter]

Emmanuelle: I may be ten years behind you, Jolivette. [Laughter]

Rosanne: We want to raise him differently than how we were raised.

Emmanuelle: He's a super sensitive kid.

Rosanne: Very!

Emmanuelle: And that's been a challenge, helping him work through all his feelings and name them [then] identify what we can let go [and] what's really a big deal to work through.

At this point of the interview, Gael wanders into the room and pops onto the computer screen.

Gael: Hi! I'm nine years old.

Jolivette: Hi Gael!

Gael waves, then leaves. We resume the conversation.

Jolivette: Do you identify your child as your son? I want to clarify that.

Emmanuelle: I do identify him as my son. I attempt when I can [to] use more gender-neutral terms so that I'm not predetermining his identity. But I do default to calling him my son.

Rosanne: I would agree. It's kind of a habit. This whole gender talk we just started having two to three years ago. Before that I didn't really understand the concept of not calling him my son.

At this, Emmanuelle nods her head in agreement.

Jolivette: Any last thoughts you'd like to add?

Emmanuelle: Can you go back to your original question?

Jolivette: About healthy masculinity? Yeah. I'm just thinking about conversations we've had in the past about wanting to help our children be able to deal with life when they grow up. To me that's based on knowing a lot of men who aren't able to deal with feelings, disappointments, or worse in a healthy way. Is there anything else you want to add about the choices you make as parents now to help them in the future?

Emmanuelle: I'm recalling our conversation! [laughs]. What's been illuminating to me about parenting is the amount of creativity and flexibility you need. It's more than I expected, and it's been a challenge, but a good challenge ... helping him identify those feelings, work through what he can do to identify if something's a big deal, or interact with his peers so his needs are met ... so he feels confident but so he's also respecting his peers, their perspectives, where they're coming from, their boundaries ... and helping him build that resilience so these comments, or "ouchies," don't build a repository of unaddressed feelings, anxieties, and resentments. Obviously, that's a work in progress for our family, but I think it's so important.

Rosanne: One of the important things for me is allowing him to have any type of emotion or sensitivity and be able to express it. I don't want to suppress a feeling he has. Because it's really important. I don't want him to feel like, *Okay, this is a gender-related feeling, let me suppress it* or *This is a feeling that boys don't have.* I want him to have his emotions and be okay with having them, [that] it's something [he's] going through. For me it's important for both of us [parents] not to suppress that or identify that [feeling] as something he shouldn't have.

Our conversation ended there, with me exclaiming that we could go on forever talking about parenting. But we saved that for future hikes and talks. In fact, six weeks later, we did reunite for another hike and talk, this time through Tilden Park in Berkeley on a typical foggy June day in the Bay Area. The boys were ten and eight this time, one on the verge of tweenhood and the other still very much a free-spirited grade-schooler. We as parents and they as children have much to learn together, but we're enjoying the meandering through the thickets and the fields.

WHERE ARE THE PRINCESS SHIRTS FOR BOYS?
by Irina González

What's underneath the surface here is that we are telling boys that it's not okay to love female characters, that it's not okay to love strong girls, that it's not okay to love women.

~Anonymous

When I found out that the sex of my baby was male, I was happy ... and also a little deflated. Like many strong women I know, I pictured myself raising a strong woman, someone who would grow up to be a little badass fighting for equality and women's rights, just like Mommy. I know how to raise a feminist girl, but how do I raise a feminist boy?

Thankfully the answer was, not much differently—I'm still raising a little badass fighting for equality and women's rights, just like Mommy, it's just that my child's sex is assigned male at birth.

One of the things that became super important to me from that day in my second trimester until now was making sure my child was exposed to all kinds of different clothes and toys, regardless of gender. But at the same time, I didn't necessarily think this meant my child could play with or wear only "gender neutral" things; in fact, I don't think that's necessary at all! Yet when it comes to making sure our kids are exposed to variety, I've found a frustrating gap between what we say is okay for girls to wear and what we deem appropriate for boys. And the way we're communicating all of this isn't good for gender equality, like, at all. Let me explain.

Where Are the Non-Pastel Gender-Neutral Clothes?

MY PARTNER AND I DECIDED to keep our baby's sex a secret until our baby shower because we really, really didn't want everything we received to be blue. But I remember being frustrated that our only other option seemed to be shades of gray.

I've heard countless complaints from fellow parents who get frustrated when adding gender-neutral things to their baby registries because those colors are just so, well, boring. If I never see another baby towel in mint green, a onesie in gray and white, or a crib sheet in pastel yellow, I'll die a happy woman. It's not necessarily that I hate those colors; I just hate the idea that our only option if we refuse to introduce our children to the "blue is for boys, pink is for girls" bullshit from birth is to buy light-colored gray and pastel clothing, sheets, and towels. What about other colors? What about non-pastel versions of those colors? What about just color diversity for both boys and girls and for everyone in between?

It's with that frame of mind that I've been buying my child clothing from both sides of the Target aisle, so to speak. He has just as many blue shirts as he has pink shirts, purple has been his favorite color ever since he could decide such things and verbalize them, and I generally approach his wardrobe with the attitude that I like fun, cute things in big, bright colors—so that's what I shop for. Though if I'm honest, I'm usually shopping in the girls' section of kids clothing stores because any gifts my child gets from loving family and friends still tend to come from the boys' section. So I joke to my partner that I'm balancing what's in our kiddo's closet and in his playroom by explicitly making sure he has things in a variety of colors. Yes, that includes pink and purple and things with flowers and designs that our society typically associates with femininity.

I'm fully committed to doing this up until the point that my child starts shopping for their own clothes—and maybe even then. I want my child to grow up and develop their own sense of style and their own sense of self, as free from societal pressures as possible. And let me tell you, it's not easy. *Everything* seems to be gendered all the damn time. This may not be a surprise to those reading this book (at least I hope not), but what's been driving me especially crazy lately is how much we tell our girls that it's okay to like "boy things" such as superheroes, but we never really tell boys that it's okay to like "girl things" such as princesses. And, as I recently discovered, we never tell boys that it's okay whether their favorite character from a popular TV show is (gasp!) a girl. Case in point was my quest to find my son a birthday shirt featuring his favorite *Paw Patrol* pup, Everest, described on the Paw Patrol website as "a female Husky pup who lives on the mountain with Jake."

Why Can't Boys Like Female TV Characters?

I THINK WE CAN ALL AGREE that, *in general*, our society is okay with teaching girls that "boy things" are okay for them, too. This isn't true in conservative circles, sure, but only the most extremist people insist that today's girls and women have to wear skirts and dresses. Women may not have bodily autonomy in the US (thanks to the overturning of *Roe v. Wade*), but at least we can wear pants.

When I walk down children's clothing aisles, everything is still very gendered when it comes to the colors and styles of clothes. But DC Comics makes a girl's Batman shirt, so we know it's okay for girls to like male characters in what has traditionally been considered a boy interest (superheroes). Overall, it's not that difficult these days to find female-gendered clothing that features both female and male characters or even just the male characters in a popular kids' television series à la any kind of superhero. But try searching for a boy's shirt from *Frozen*, a favorite movie of my son's, and you'll find a gray shirt featuring Olaf. And while I think the silly talking snowman is adorable, why can't I find a boy's *Frozen* shirt that features, I dunno, the two actual leading characters of the movie—sisters Elsa and Anna—without also featuring two male characters?

It seems the only option for male children who love female-led movies and TV is to buy from the girls' section of the store. And while I know that using "boy" and "girl" in this context is problematic, I also know that this is the reality we live in. Every store tells us to pick a side to shop in based not on what our child likes but on what it says on their birth certificate.

Deconstructing all of this is important for sure. But in the meantime, we need to start teaching boys that it's awesome that their favorite character from *Moana* is, ahem, MOANA, and not the chicken or the demigod. If a girl's *Moana* shirt can solely feature a secondary male character, then why can't a boy's *Moana* shirt solely feature the leading character who happens to be female?

This is endlessly frustrating to me.

And it's all coming to a head right now because my child's birthday party is coming up, and I cannot find a themed birthday shirt for him that features his favorite character from *Paw Patrol*. Why? Because she happens to be a girl, so all the shirts featuring her say "Birthday Girl." *Birthday girl!* Why can't it be "Birthday Pup" (which is available only for the primary female character) or something that doesn't bring gender into this at all? I'm not even saying "Birthday Person" because that might look a bit odd on a kid's birthday shirt, but a simple "It's My 4th Birthday" on a shirt that features the secondary female pup would suffice.

Making Rainbows Out of Pink and Blue

SO WHAT AM I TO DO?

Well, despite gender being a social construct, I don't necessarily want to confuse people by having my son wear a "birthday girl" shirt. On the one hand, who cares? It's just a cute shirt with his favorite puppy, am I right? But on the other hand, we do still live in this gendered society, and there are still some gender lines I am very comfortable standing on top of but not crossing just yet. So, for lack of a better idea—and because I am determined not to let society tell my son that his favorite character can't be female—I bought him the shirt and plan to use fabric paint to turn that "girl" into a "kid"! It's not going to look perfect, but hopefully it'll look decent enough.

I feel like I'm doing two things at once here, both trying to subvert gendered expectations and still adhering to them a bit. Look, it's a complicated issue, and I don't have all the answers. I have only what feels right(ish) to me right now, and this is it.

At the end of the day, what I really hope to communicate with my child's birthday girl/kid shirt is that he's allowed to love a female character most of all *and* that he's allowed to express that publicly—as all kids should be!

We're never going to find true equality between the sexes until we encourage men to embrace their feminine sides as much as we're already encouraging women to embrace their masculine sides. I mean, it would be super-duper great if we could just *not* gender things like color and personality traits, but that's a bigger mountain to climb for another time. In the meantime, I hope we all take a pause and think about how truly fucked up it is that if you search for a *Peppa Pig* shirt for boys, you'll find one featuring her brother George. At the end of the day, what's underneath the surface here is that we are telling boys that it's not okay to love female characters, that it's not okay to love strong girls, that it's not okay to love women. And isn't that a huge part of the problem? I certainly think so.

Teaching children things like gender equality and consent doesn't happen just through words. It happens through actions, too. And subtle actions like not having princess shirts for boys tells them there is something wrong with having an affinity for princesses, which translates to there being something wrong with loving female characters, which translates to female characters not being worthy of their love and respect. And it's not that many steps down the incel road after that when the primary message we're sending here is that female characters are not worthy of male admiration.

So please, let's bring on the princess shirts for boys. Let's tell them that it's awesome they love an animated puppy who happens to be female. Let's encourage them to wear pink and jump in muddy puddles just like Peppa.

While we're at it, let's shut down all these things that subtly tell our boys not to respect women. After all, isn't that what needs to happen for us to truly raise little badass kids fighting for equality and women's rights? Yes, I would say it is.

THE ULTIMATE ACT OF DEFIANCE
by Robin Lowey

Raising two sons in a lesbian household is the ultimate act of defiance. Fuck the patriarchy!

The funny thing is, my thinking didn't start out this way. It's something that came to me in the lucky way that someone gets exactly what they never wanted yet it turns out to be the greatest thing ever.

One of my earliest memories is standing in front of a mirror, flexing my eight-year-old skinny tomboy arms and declaring to myself, "I will never marry a man! I will never have a baby!" Had I understood there was an option, I no doubt would have chosen to be a nonbinary child. Fast forward through all the disillusionments I endured from being born female, the systematic dismantling of my bravado. I was a rough-and-tumble kid denied a spot on the Little League team (the law changed six years after my time) who seemingly overnight turned into a classically beautiful, statuesque blonde. I knew deep down I was gay but convinced myself I was straight. I liked boys and they liked me. I was soon "discovered" and began a brief modeling career, landing in *Playboy* and *Penthouse* at age 19. The predatory attention I received was terrifying. More than once after I spurned a man's unwanted advances, they called me a dyke.

I held onto my childhood vow about no marriage or children, even after I came out as a lesbian in my early 20s. It was my then-partner, Pam—with whom I spent the following 27 years—who taught me about feminism. This took time and effort because even though I had many firsthand experiences with sexism, I was somehow in denial about the patriarchal oppression of women! I was *so* angry but had nothing I could pin it on. I'm forever indebted to Pam for unwinding my denial and helping me change my thinking. She turned me on to women's music and gave me books to read. Listening to Olivia Records's *Lesbian Concentrate* and reading books such as Rita Mae Brown's *Plain Brown Wrapper* kickstarted my education on feminism. What a relief to finally begin to understand why the world did not make sense to me and how sexism and the imbalance of power hurts us all, men and women alike.

Then, after seven years together, Pam decided she wanted to have kids, with or without me. It was 1989, and this idea was not on my radar at all. Dykes don't have children … do they? She was going to get pregnant, and it was nonnegotiable. *Whaaaat?!* I actually considered leaving her. I slept on a friend's uncomfortable couch for a week and finally came to the realization that I really loved Pam and that if this was what she wanted I would just have to adjust my thinking … again!

We began the process by attending a workshop based on Cheri Pies's 1985 book *Considering Parenthood: A Workbook for Lesbians.* These workshops were a lifeline for lesbians who wanted to have children but needed help navigating the practical and legal issues around adoption, the use of sperm donors, HIV, and more. I remember the scariest part for me was creating a pie chart that clearly showed we would have only a tiny sliver of time left for ourselves after our child was born. *Why would anybody in their right mind want a child?* I wondered. It became clear to me that this could never be a rational decision for anyone. Lesbians, who had to jump through hoops to make a pregnancy happen, had to really want children! And that, in and of itself, set us apart from many straight couples who stumbled on parenthood accidentally.

I breathed a sigh of relief when I found out that the average time to get pregnant using alternative insemination was eight months. This would give me time to prepare myself; besides, we still had to find a donor. I figured I had at least two years before this little punk would disrupt our lives. Then, out of the blue, we got a call from my brother's wife, offering him up as a sperm donor! My bro and I are very close, and he already had a kid of his own, so it seemed like a great idea. I was surprised to learn that this turkey baster thing was nonsense. I inseminated Pam with a tiny syringe, and voilà! Our son Max was born nine months later.

In 1990, we were advised to enter "unknown" in the

space for "father" on the birth certificate, after which we had to go see a judge at city hall so I could formally adopt Max. This meant Pam had to give up her legal rights as the mother. The gray-haired judge admonished us, wagging his finger and saying, "Are you sure you want to give up your child to this woman?" Our lawyer advised us that the adoption was a workaround and that the birth mother would indeed be able to retain her rights. This was some scary uncharted territory we were dealing with here.

Eventually, we petitioned successfully to get my name on the birth certificate too. We were now the proud parents of Max, a sweet, good-natured, and agreeable boy who almost immediately slept through the night and brought us endless joy. I used to wonder why other parents were so sleep-deprived or why they "let" their children scream.

On our first outing with Max when he was three weeks old, an older woman approached the stroller and said, "Oh my, his father must be so proud!" It felt awkward, and we didn't know how to respond. We started to wonder how we might best parent this boy. We wanted to make sure he grew up to be a feminist and a loving, nurturing man.

Later on, he was playing with a piece of toast and pretended it was a gun. *Bang bang!* We were concerned and we went to a lesbian therapist about it; she advised us to stop worrying so much. He loved baseball, the beach, baking cookies, and his sparkly gem collection. When he asked Santa for an Easy Bake Oven for Christmas, we were delighted. It came only in Barbie pink, but we didn't mind, and neither did he. When we marched in the stroller brigade at the Gay Pride Parade in San Francisco, Max shouted, "Happy Gay Day!" to the crowd. He especially loved "all the pretty ladies in high heels" we saw marching around us.

We decided we didn't want an only child, so after a few years, Pam began insemination with sperm we had saved from my brother. By then he had two kids and a recent vasectomy, so we had a limited supply. We tried intrauterine insemination, but Pam had secondary infertility and it just didn't work. I decided to step in and try to get pregnant myself with an anonymous donor from the sperm bank. It was now 1995, and the laws made it a little easier to co-parent a child as a same-sex couple. I got pregnant right away, and although I absolutely hated every minute of my pregnancy, I found the act of giving birth to be the most empowering and profound thing I've ever experienced. I felt like an Amazon warrior!

That was until I realized I had produced a very difficult little screamer who could not self-soothe or sleep more than a couple of hours at a time. Max had fooled us into thinking parenting was a relatively easy proposition. Those were most certainly the hardest and most sleep-deprived years of my life. I cried every day. But when Sam started school, everything changed, and he became a model student. Sam will never be seen as "compliant"; he is a critical thinker who stands up for what he believes in. He has always been a leader and a self-possessed young man who sets his mind to things and makes them happen.

Although our boys spent most of their childhood around our pack of lesbian friends, they had many good men in their lives while growing up, all of whom brought much to the table for them to learn from. My brother is still a loving uncle, and my dad was a loving "papa." We often spent time with heterosexual "Lezbros," gay male friends, and other kids' dads. The boys also had many male sports coaches and teachers. Even so, we took a lot of heat from folks asking if we had proper male role models. I have to admit that we had spent a fair amount of time thinking and worrying about this issue. Ultimately, the boys had two loving parents who brought different interests and ways of parenting to the table. Besides, the whole world is predominantly male-centric, so I feel confident the boys received plenty of male influence.

Our boys grew up in a female-centric home, learning to communicate well, express their feelings, and be kind and helpful to others. Max participated in Peggy Drexler's study that became the book *Raising Boys without Men,* and he was interviewed periodically over the course of several years when he was young. I'm proud that my son contributed to the premise Dr. Drexler proved that sons of lesbians have a strong moral compass equal to or surpassing their peers from heterosexual families. It's not at all surprising to me.

If we had reservations about bringing boys into the world, we quickly learned that producing two heterosexual white male allies is very powerful in terms of changing society. We made it a point to instill in them the understanding of their position of privilege, how they have had so much handed to them, and that their successes are not solely based on how great or smart they are. Plus, they have been witnesses to our lives, including the sexism in our careers, the sexual harassment, and the fact that we always seemed to make less money than families with heterosexual parents.

There were many moments when the boys showed their ability to navigate the world in their own unique ways. When we first moved to the suburbs from San Francisco, when Max was 10 years old, he was surprised to hear, "You're so gay!" shouted out in the schoolyard. We explained to him that we weren't in San Francisco anymore and that the people in this town were ignorant. As the new kid, he took a stand and told these kids he wouldn't be their friend if they spoke that way because his parents were gay and it was a good thing. It worked out, and he became a popular kid with many friends.

Max has since grown into a strong feminist and vocal advocate for LGBTQIA+ rights. At 34, he is a successful engineer living in Monterey County. When my friends and I marched in the first Women's March in San Francisco in our pink pussy hats a few years ago, I unexpectedly ran into Max. He and his roommate had come to the march on their own volition, and I was surprised and thrilled to see him. I had an extra pink hat, and he wore it proudly that day. His choices show me that activism and feminism are in his bones. Max gets it.

At 28, Sam is an adventurous world traveler, a lover of nature, and an incredibly talented writer. He is my biggest champion and an advisor to my work on the Lesbian Game Changers project. He not only crafted the foreword for this very book but has demonstrated his passion for racial and gender equity, LGBTQIA+ rights, and feminism in so many ways. Currently, Sam is the director of communications at Shooting Touch, a nonprofit organization in Rwanda that uses basketball to provide roughly 3,000 youth and women with essential physical, social, and mental health education and resources. In response to the deeply rooted patriarchal systems existing in rural Rwanda, Shooting Touch ensures equal opportunity on the basketball courts and helps reshape harmful gender norms and social structures that are holding women and girls back from reaching their highest potential.

There is a paradigm shift beginning to happen in our culture, and raising boys in lesbian households contributes to that shift. I'm seeing traditionally masculine behaviors such as being powerful, proactive, and ambitious becoming more and more acceptable in women. Conversely, traditional feminine values such as vulnerability, being collaborative, and nurturing are now becoming sought-after qualities in *all* people.

It seems less likely that members of the oppressed group will change the status quo; real change will occur when our allies (and children) push against societal norms. How lucky am I, a person who was certain she would never have children, to have had the privilege of enjoying being a parent and giving birth.

Raising boys is indeed the ultimate act of feminist defiance. My sons are my biggest contribution to changing the world.

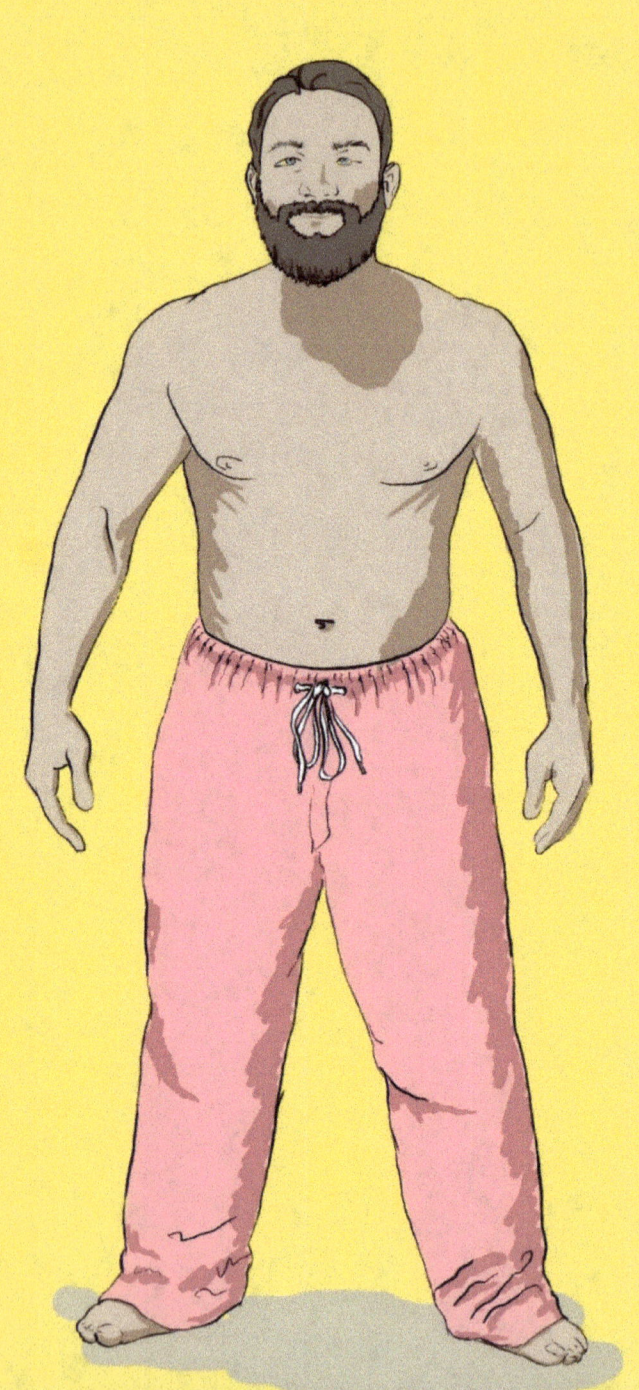

INTERVIEW: SABRINA WHITE
by Gail Marlene Schwartz

I met Sabrina White when I was teaching writing at the Community College of Vermont. Sabrina had attended CCV years ago, and when I met her, her son was enrolling. When she learned about *Reimagining Boyhood*, she was eager to participate. I recorded our interview and then edited the transcript with Sabrina's permission. What follows are her words.

I'M DEFINITELY A RECOVERING Catholic. It's built into your mind that this is the way you live. There's a man and a woman, and you get married once. It was this perfect family idea that's put into your head at a young age and reinforced constantly.

My dad had a nervous breakdown when I was seven or eight, and he never really recovered. He never worked again, and he survived on disability. He wasn't an active parent because he was in and out of the VA home when he got depressed. The structural part of my upbringing was from my mother, who looked at the world from a black and white place. Because she wore the pants in the family (though she didn't believe it), she was a total hypocrite. She would complain about how people didn't take her seriously, and this was in the 1970s. I used to think about how unfair that was. My mom could do anything; she ran a business and paid the bills. Our house was a little shabby, but our lives improved over time.

I had one older sister, and she was a wild child. I was the good kid. I was seven years younger than my sister, who had a lot of influence on me. She took care of me while Mom was working. I'd spend whole days with my sister, especially in summer. She dropped out of school and moved away at [age] 18, then came home, [and] she passed away when she was 27. During my four years of high school, my sister was sick, and my mom was gone visiting her in the hospital; she would work at the bakery, then go to the hospital. I took on lots of responsibility being alone a lot.

From age 10 or 11, I knew I had gender feelings that were different. I was definitely interested in what it would be like to be the other gender. I never felt like, "This is a boy's job, this is a girl's job." I don't really have words to describe it. I'd put it in the back of my mind, not think about it too much, but the thoughts were always there. When you go through puberty, the sexuality piece is there.

The thought of being a woman made me feel sexual. Part of that was taboo; it was exciting.

After high school, I met my first wife. We were young, dumb, and horny. We had two kids—a girl, Amanda, and a boy, Zack—both unplanned, but we were married by the time we had the second one. They are 30 and 31 now. I was married to [my first wife] for nine years, and I definitely felt like I was both Mom and Dad in that family. She never breastfed … I remember getting up with the kids, changing them. Zack had autism, and it was a lot of work, very stressful. All through this time, gender dysphoria was in my mind. I had a secret stash of clothes and dress[ed] up, but it was always for short periods of time. I thought that maybe it was a fetish thing; I would think, *I don't have to tell anyone. I can keep it a secret.* At that time, I knew there were trans people, but we didn't have the internet, so there was no way to research it; I didn't get a computer until 1999.

Eventually, I came out to my first wife. She seemed fine with it. We'd put the kids to bed and [then] I'd dress up as a female, but our marriage was a mess. I think anybody who gets married at 20 is doomed. We grew apart. She didn't care what I was doing; she was using the computer, was in chat groups, and eventually connected with someone online and was unfaithful. I didn't want to believe that happened because I was trans; I rejected the whole trans thing. When I got divorced, I worked it out with my ex-wife that we had joint custody … they stayed with me during the school year; I had them 70 percent of the time. This was unusual for dads back then.

Because I felt different, like an outlier, I was always

open-minded, always battling my upbringing: My mom was racist [and] homophobic, all those things, and still is (though she says she's not). I rejected those ideas and instilled acceptance and openness in my kids.

I got married to Katie, my second wife, when I was 31, and we've been married for 23 years. We had a son, Hayden, together, and she helped me raise [my] other two. She was only 26 when I met her, so there's an age difference. She hadn't had many relationships and is very career-driven. Katie is a totally different person [from] my first wife. We are the perfect nerd match; we fit together great. Katie isn't a nurturing mom. Talk about spouses; I married a wife who's a man! She's unemotional and she doesn't talk a lot. She's great. We've actually never had an argument! We've never even raised our voices. I've always been the nurturing parent in our family.

There are two halves of my life. Before I worked at a hospital, I owned European Autoworks. That was my first career. When I quit that, I sold my partnership and went to school, and that was a huge switch of who I was. I went from blue-collar to white-collar work—computer work. It went with the gender change. For the first five years of marriage, I repressed the trans piece of my identity. I was so in love with Katie [and] would push that aside.

Then I got tired of the shop. I went back to school, which meant long drives to Williston, the Vermont Technical College campus, and that gave me time to think about things and who I was. That gave me the time to think about what I wanted in life. I'd think, *What if I [were] "Sabrina"?* At first it didn't seem possible, but then I got to know more and more people, people [who] liked me in my new life, which made it easier. Women are so much more accepting of allowing people to be who they are. Education also makes a big difference because you see the world a bit wider.

Before I transitioned, people could tell I wasn't happy and [and] hard to live with. I used certain hobbies as a buffer in my mind. I just shut down. When I went out in public, it would bother me more. I felt awkward. I didn't like myself. When I was home with the family, it was much easier to not think about it. But out in public, I was seeing other women, thinking, *I wish I could express myself that way, be more naturally myself.* It really affected everyone around me.

I fully transitioned three years ago. I told Katie 10 years ago; it's been a slow journey. My daughter Amanda is the oldest and the one I was closest to at that time, so I told her first. At that time, when I first started pushing the boundaries and telling people in my immediate family, I had in my mind [that] I could have two selves. I'd spend some time as Sabrina and some time as my male self. I'd pretend. I found a trans group in southern New Hampshire and started getting out every month. My daughter was in college, and we'd meet [up and] spend the day in Burlington. I told her verbally. She said to me, "Oh, that's why you're so depressed all the time."

Katie has told me in the last few years that she enjoys living with a happier person. Deep down inside, I think she wouldn't have minded if I stayed the other way. But she understands I had to do it to be happy even though she lost something along the way. So because of that, it made her happier. But it was really a big change. I [was] always amazed that she seem[ed] comfortable with it. In that relationship, we were intimate for a while after I came out, but it became harder for her. She would tell me, "I'm not a lesbian." So now we're platonic. That's one of the few things that makes me feel sad; there's a little bit of mourning for that piece. We love each other a lot, but we don't express it that way. The intimacy [has] changed.

My mom won't use my new name. She tries to use my old (male) name, or sometimes she works around it; she won't say any name. She definitely won't use the right pronouns. I avoid going to see her except if she needs help. I do get tired of just talking about the weather. We can't talk about anything real. She falls into that conspiracy baloney, like with Fox News. As a Catholic, she thinks the pope is God's representative on Earth and the Bible is the word of God. Actually, the current pope knows that the world isn't black and white. He gets that doctrine doesn't matter; it's about being good to one another. When I told my mom that the pope isn't condemning LGBTQIA+ people, she said, "The pope is an asshole."

Zack, my older son, told me he doesn't have a problem with my being trans, but I think it's harder for him internally. Right now, we have a rough relationship. He will call me up [and be] all nice, then try to say things that will bother me. I think he does it to get attention. He was doing that before I transitioned, but it's worse now. It's been harder for him to get along with me. He [is also] jealous of Hayden, [who] is from [my] second marriage, and he thought Hayden was spoiled.

Amanda's been trying to adjust. She calls me "T-mom" (trans mom). I transitioned late in life, so I'm happy to take what I can get.

Hayden either calls me Mom or T-mom. I told him I wasn't going to put a lot of pressure on him because I don't want anything to be forced. Nothing bothers me more than forcing something on someone.

At work, if someone misgenders me, unless there's clear intent, I don't take offense. I look at everything that way. People get too hung up ... the cancel culture thing is so destructive. Many aren't intending to hurt by saying the wrong thing, and we can't help the culture we're brought up in. As long as we try to be a little better to one another every day, that's all that really matters. Nobody is perfect.

Hayden is slow to change on anything. Over the last three years, I [have] said, "You can call me 'Dad' at home, but in public it's 'Sabrina' or 'Mom.' Don't say 'Dad' in public." He cares. I can definitely see it. He'll apologize if he makes a mistake in public, and I definitely don't want to make him feel bad. It goes back to that intent issue: He didn't ask for his dad to be trans. I don't think he viewed my transition as a loss, like he was losing a dad, even though he didn't know until four years ago. I've been a lot more myself over the last 10 years in many ways.

I've influenced Hayden a lot. I've tried to instill fairness ... but not just fairness. From a feminist side, I've tried to show him the idea that men and women are different but equal. He now looks at the world like this.

If he [ever] said anything chauvinistic, I'd shoot it down right away. Out in the world, I'd be so upset when men would talk disgustingly about women and make all these assumptions. Sometimes I'd say something ... it was a long time ago. I wouldn't necessarily respond, but I also wouldn't join in. I would sort of go quiet. It's hard. Peer pressure is hard; male peer pressure is hard. [But] I tried to always let my kids know how important it was to understand the world and see the bigger picture. We are not just Americans. Nothing is that black and white. Not all cultures look at things the same. Indigenous cultures look at gender differently than other cultures.

My older son Zack considers himself bisexual. He'll wear pink Hello Kitty pajama bottoms, but he's a big hairy guy with a full beard and [is] totally comfortable with that. I allowed him to do what he wanted when he was growing up. He liked some of that [dressing feminine] as a kid, and I never shunned him for it.

Hayden is solid in being a cisgender male. He's not macho, though. I've never heard him say anything disrespectful of women or talk about physical weakness. He just assumes a woman can do what a man can do and vice versa; there are no limits. I think this comes out of his parenting—both of us. Even though Katie is all female and she looks feminine, she's strong. She won't avoid lifting something because it's too heavy. [And] nobody says, "That's a woman's job." It's never been said in my house.

I do see a difference between the older two and Hayden: Hayden grew up later, and going through school was better. Zack got along great with my mom; he listened to her. A lot of stuff she said was baloney, but he heard it over and over again. He has "This is how a family should look" in his brain. He thinks that there's this ideal family model out there somewhere. I say, "Good luck"; usually, the ideal family is the one that scares me the most because they have the biggest secrets. Zack works at a gas station, one that gets truckers and farmers. He sits and bullshits with those guys all day. I think he's reverted because of that influence. It [has] strained our relationship a bit. It makes it harder for him to be accepting.

With Hayden, Katie and I were united in raising him. He's more of an academic; he loves history, science, and psychology, [and] he reads and watches documentaries. His view of the world is wider. Amanda has lots of schooling also; she's a therapist. With Hayden, I feel like emotionally I'm more open. When he gets upset, I can empathize with it better and show it. Even good dads say, "You're a boy, be strong." [But] I don't do that to him. I didn't do it before [I transitioned] … From growing up in an adverse childhood, I understand that life is tough. Sometimes you have to let yourself fall apart and feel it. If you try too hard to say, "I'm going to be strong," you push it into a hidden place where it will bite you down the road. I encourage [my kids] to express themselves, and much more so since my transition.

During the last part of my life before I transitioned, I was dead emotionally. It was just about getting through every day. Life gets tiring that way. Now I'm getting to be close to women at work. Those relationships are so different. I have a few friends, [but at] my age [and] as a trans woman, it's hard to relate …. I tend to get along with the younger crowd; they are nurses in their 30s having kids. That's what they're talking about. I have a harder time hanging out with women in their 40s. One friend I'm close to who is just a bit younger, we're in that same place in life. We talk about everything—like our mothers and how impossible they are. We share that, and I get a lot out of that. "I don't even see you as that old person at all," [she says]. In her mind, I'm a woman.

A SET OF TOO-PRETTY SHEETS
by Devon Ward

"It's too pretty!" howled my son Cary, his fingers tracing over the flower pattern on the sheet I had just put on.

The night was not going well. He's got asthma, and at bedtime he coughed so forcefully he threw up his dinner into his bed. My older son, Sam, who sleeps on the bottom bunk, was so curious and determined to help that he was perpetually in the way. I needed a distraction, so I called my ex-wife, their other parent, on the phone. But of course, now she was overhearing all of this. I hate that. I hate feeling like I can't handle everything as a single mom. I hate needing her help in any capacity. Even having her on the phone while I clean up vomit feels like a failure to my identity as an independent, single mom who doesn't need anything from anybody.

Then, on top of that, Cary wouldn't get into his bed

because the only spare sheet I had in the house had flowers on it and they were "too pretty." Trying not to laugh, I explained to him that I didn't have any uglier sheets and needed him to lie down. It was well past his bedtime, and he had school in the morning, assuming he was well enough.

A day or two later, my ex called and said, "When he said it was 'too pretty,' what he meant was 'too girly.' What have we done wrong?"

THE ANSWER IS FAIRLY obvious: At ages four and five, both my boys have started school, and all the carefully curated ideas about gender that we've been providing them are now out of our hands. From this point on, it's not us who have the final say in who they are; it's a group of 25 or so kids who are also spending six hours a day in the kindergarten classrooms of the school up the street. I'm sure they're very trustworthy as a group, but I went to a birthday party recently and watched one of them get stuck trying to slide backward down an inflatable. Now they are building one another's identities? Seems like a big ask.

It's the surprising things that are tripping me up. Cary is refusing to wear a coat because he wants to look "cool" at school (being a comfortable body temperature is obviously for losers), and he won't put his shoulder-length hair in a ponytail because that's for girls (Sam's hair is longer than mine, but for some reason that doesn't seem to be a problem). Sam earnestly explained that he has to pee standing up at school because that's what boys do, although he still sits when he's at home. They are both constantly misgendered out in the world because they have chosen to keep their hair long. Sam also loves the color purple, shirts with traditionally feminine patterns, and leggings that tend to fit his tall, skinny frame better. But even if he's wearing baggy sweatpants and a construction sweater, he's misgendered. For him, it doesn't seem to matter. Sometimes he corrects people and sometimes he doesn't. Cary is more consistent with identifying himself as a boy when someone gets it wrong.

When I was picking up Sam from daycare last year, there was a big poster asking everyone to guess what sex a teacher's baby would be—pink soothers on one side and blue on the other. Sam asked me about it, and I explained. Then he asked, "Which one is for girl, and which one is for boy?" I asked him to look at the letters and guess, and he figured out the difference between "g" and "b." We never once talked about how pink is for girls and blue is for boys.

I'm fairly sure that was the best my parenting will ever get, and it's all downhill from there. Now I watch them play. My long-haired, purple-shirted, pink-unicorn-sheet-preferring child builds, engineers, and is all about the construction and destruction of towers, buildings, and pipelines (never mind masculinity; how did I raise a child who's pro-pipeline?). My too-cool-for-flowers-on-his-sheets son cradles his beloved stuffed bunny gently in his arms and explains that his bunny was calling for his mommy but is okay now because he is the mommy. I want so desperately for these organic, nonbinary elements to slowly grow into their souls. I want them to know that we are all both masculine and feminine, that they aren't a dichotomy but a garden, one that is wild, changing, beautiful, nurturing, strong, open, and meant to be shared.

Maybe every parent who's ever lived has looked into the future sometime around 2:30 a.m. when they're exhausted but sitting up holding a sleeping head against their heart, pressing kisses into the hair, and tickling the cheek. I have, anyway, more times than I can count. I am full of hope and dreams, wishes and desperate prayers—sometimes to no one—for a good future that will somehow be intangibly *better* than the present. Maybe every parent has looked back at their mistakes and their failings and wondered how they ended up here, worried about how they can keep those mistakes from hurting the little one asleep in their lap.

When my marriage ended, it was a hard time for me and for my kids. I sobbed to a therapist one day that I didn't know how I was supposed to explain the world to them. Slowly we talked through it until I found myself saying, "I have to trust the strength of my relationship with my kids." Trust in a scary world. Trust that they can hold onto who they are, trust that whenever the world tries to pull them into two distinct pieces for the purpose of killing the feminine half, they will know they can come to me. They will know I can help them repair the damage to their souls, gently ease both parts back together, and weave them into each other where they belong.

I don't know whether I'm the perfect person to do this. I am a product of a binary worldview: I'm a good mom, or I'm not. I'm a capable single parent, or I'm not. There's not a lot of nuance in my mind for myself.

But I have to learn, for them.

Because I'm not sure the opposite of toxic masculinity is healthy masculinity. I think it's understanding that there isn't an opposite, there's only wholeness, which is inherently resistant to dichotomy. They deserve to be whole as little kids and as whomever they grow into. I trust they will.

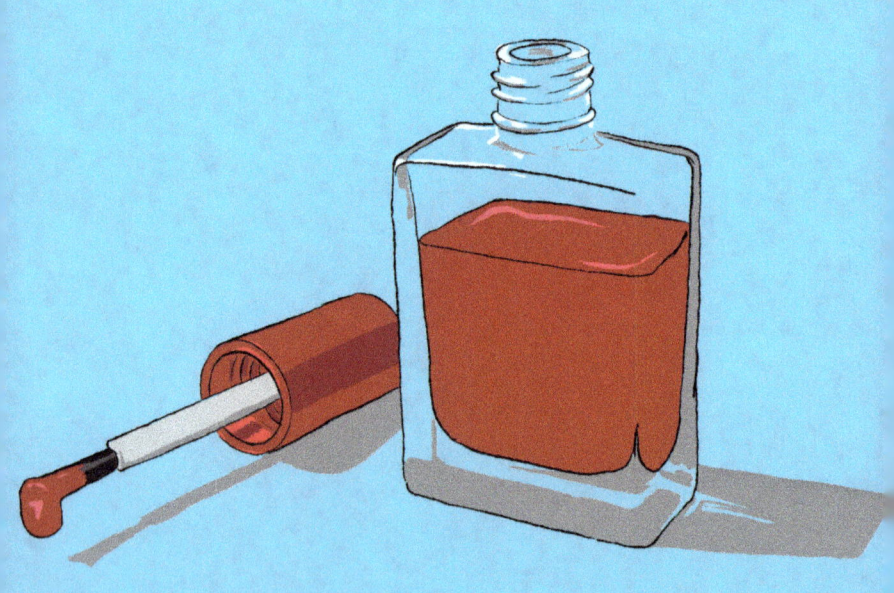

INTERVIEW: BROOKE STRAUSS
by Ada Malone

Brooke and Rita Strauss have a son, River, who is seven years old, and a daughter, Remy, who is three and a half. Brooke and I had overlapping pregnancies with our sons being born just three months apart. We've had many conversations over the years about parenting gentle boys and about our boys growing up surrounded by not only our queer families but also those hetero families that inevitably become a part of your lives once you have kids.

I interviewed Brooke more formally about this topic via Zoom in November of 2021. Here are some of her insights on raising a feminist boy in world that is not always so welcoming of feminism nor queerness. These are Brooke's words based on the transcript and edited by me with her permission.

On Being a Good Human Regardless of Gender

IN A GENERAL SENSE, we're raising River to be a good human being and also supporting those general traits and a sense of masculinity that in some ways is a part of him or will be a part of him later on.

On Consent

IN TERMS OF RAISING HIM to be nonsexist, we've talked a lot about consent in general. We don't always call it consent, but we're trying to do a lot of work around that with him. It starts with his own body, wanting him to feel empowered with his own body choices, his own right to his body. We tell him we need to check with people before we touch their bodies, so he's had a lot of intentional work around consent from a very young age. Lately I've been noticing that if I give him a hug without asking and he's not really into it, I tell him, "You know, you can tell me if you don't want me to hug you. That's okay."

River is an incredibly affectionate and warm child with the four of us, but he's not that way with other people. My parents always want to hug and kiss; it's just expected. And from the time River was little, I could tell he just wasn't comfortable with that. So we try to be proactive. At the time, I'll say, "Let's greet Grandma and Grandpa, but it's up to you how you want to greet them. These are your options, the different ways you can greet them depending on your comfort level." I think my parents understand that … I know they still secretly want hugs and kisses, but I think they're mindful of the larger message.

On the Importance of Modeling and Normalizing Feelings and Queerness

WE TRY TO MAKE HIM comfortable talking about his feelings. We tell him that talking about emotions is important and healthy. And it's not only teaching that but also modeling that every day.

We also try to demonstrate being wrong, being able to say, "I'm sorry." I think society makes it harder for men to say they're sorry. It's part of honoring River's own innate sensitivity. I think that can be viewed as something negative for boys or men, so we're trying to honor that and recognize what an innate strength that is for him.

Rita has a super queer family, not only with sexual orientation but also with the gender identity and expression of her siblings and her nieces, so [queerness is] modeled very much as the norm. It has opened up a lot of conversations very naturally and easily, such as, "Uncle Greg's partner" and "that's his boyfriend." River's cousins are transgender, so there's a lot of opportunity for an ongoing conversation, which has been great. I think that exposure leads to fewer set expectations for him [as far as] who he is or his gender identity and someday who he's attracted to. It's having the message early on that all of it is okay, that you are you, and that what feels right to each person is different.

I think once they get to this age, it's not only modeling but also being able to have dialogue and conversations about what River is noticing or what's out there in the world. Last year [for instance], some kids were asking him, "Where's your dad? Do you have a dad?" We had a conversation with his teacher to be proactive with Father's Day and also so she [could] know how we talked to River about it, so if she noticed it was coming up in school, she could use the language that we used. We wanted her to be able to help support River with that. When we first started out, during the first few years of [his] life, we would tell him, "You know you have two moms and a donor … you don't have a dad." And that's shifted for us in the past few years. Now it's like, "Actually, you have a biological father." Because that's the reality, he does have a biological father. It's not someone who's in his life every day or will be, at least now.

On the Men in River's Life

HE DOES HAVE UNCLES who are involved, not in his daily life but that he sees. He also has two grandfathers who are active and involved, and neither of [them] are what society would consider to be super masculine men … which we love and appreciate. They fall into certain masculine traps or expectations, but they're not super rough and tough men, which is great for [River] to see.

On Judaism and Defying Societal Expectations

THEN THERE'S JUDAISM. We haven't really practiced too much of the religious components, more of the cultural components, but I think we've also pushed against some of the more cultural expectations of Judaism with boys. For example, in Judaism there's this expectation that you circumcise your son, and we were very much against that. We felt it was his body and should be his choice, not ours. This goes against what my family has historically done to baby boys, so that was something that was really important to us and continues to be.

We haven't had the conversation of intact versus circumcised penises yet. He hasn't come to us saying, "Why does [so-and-so's] penis look like that?" But we're always talking about how bodies are so different, that some can be very similar, some can be very different, and that's all okay. I think it's important [to] make choices for yourself and your children that push against the norm or society's expectations.

The biggest thing we've been trying to do is just letting him be who he is and supporting that, letting that develop and grow versus putting our or society's kind of expectations on him. We've tried to encourage some of the traits that might be considered less masculine. And I think that goes back to maybe the intentional piece. We're trying to defy gender expectations. We don't want to just go along with what's expected in society or what society is telling us. I think we try to challenge how society views masculinity and point it out when we can. We also try to model some level of vulnerability or let him know that it's okay to be vulnerable, it's okay to cry, it's okay to have feelings. We want to really normalize that because boys, even at the age of seven, are getting messages from outside the home that it's not okay.

Remy was really excited about getting a nail polish kit for her third birthday, and she was painting everyone's nails: ours, Grandpa's, our neighbors', and dogs'. So with River, we were like, "Do you want to get your nails done too?" There was a little pause, but then he decided he wanted to have his nails painted. And he saw that I got my nails done, and our neighbor—who's a self-identified man—got his nails done, so all that modeling was really, really important. I also had to have a conversation with him because he was going to school. I said that anyone, no matter what gender identity they are, can wear nail polish. And I said, "But what's silly and kind of sad is that sometimes people think this is only for girls." I wanted to prepare him and to know what he would say if someone came up to him and noticed his nails and said he couldn't wear it. I wanted him to have the words of how he could respond if that came up.

Well, it did come up. A girl in his class the next day said, "You know you're a boy. Why are you wearing nail polish?" [River] was able to verbalize, "It's because I want to. Anyone can wear it." [It was] great that he had the words and was able to verbalize [them], but he has never worn nail polish [since]. Clearly he's getting the message from society, even from kids his own age, that boys are expected to be a certain way, so we're trying to balance that out at home.

It's been interesting in elementary school just seeing what he's drawn to, like with clothes ... and he's really into sports. He's currently obsessed with baseball, and he wants to be watching it all the time. So we let him watch professional baseball games and go to baseball games with him, and [we notice] so many of the things he's observing and taking in around him—for better or worse—and we're just like *Oh my gosh* ... and then [see him] kind of reenact that himself.

On Queer Mom "Fails"

RITA HAD BROUGHT A bunch of old files to work that she was shredding, and there were two or three reports from our daycare [full] of developmental milestones of River when he was a baby. So she took them out and didn't shred them, and we [went] through them. The teachers [had reported] on things they felt he needed to work on. He must have been about a year old, and they were saying that whenever one of the dads came in the room, he got scared. We were like, "Oh, is that a queer mom fail?"

Another thing was when one of the other kids would take a toy out of his hand and River couldn't care less; the teachers were trying to work with him on saying no. We didn't care. We actually thought it [was] good that he [was] not bopping someone over the head because they grabbed his toy. But the teachers were like, "You've got to stand up for yourself and take that toy back; be a boy," which was kind of how we interpreted it.

I struggle with that. Like, I'm noticing he wants to be doing typical boy things now. He's so into sports, he's always been very physically developed and steady on speed, and he has very strong physical abilities. So it comes very naturally to him. Of course I want to support his interest and desire to be physically active. We noticed it from the beginning. During the first few years, we were [saying], "Let's get you into gymnastics," and trying different activities to let him use his body, [such as] swimming, gymnastics, and soccer. Now he's very drawn to baseball. So how much of that do we allow him to watch and absorb from society? Because I think he really identifies with it.

OVERALL, BROOKE AND Rita rely on modeling to counter the daily societal messages that River is getting about what boyhood and masculinity look like. While they go outside their comfort zones a bit in supporting River in his interests, which look so stereotypically male, they also create space and conversation about the version of masculinity that matters to them.

MARRIAGE AND FAMILY
by Amy Hinze-Pifer

I was raised as a gender fundamentalist. My parents are religious, but the true gospel of my childhood was the nuclear family.

Our gendered world was organized around family roles. The core was the nuclear family, which consists of one man, one woman, and enough but not too many children. The father role is held by a man, and everything will go terribly wrong if it isn't. The father is the head of the household and provides stability in exchange for absolute deference. The mother role is held by a woman because women have special gifts and talents for caregiving that are valued as long as they're provided for free. The mother is the heart and the hands of the family but never the voice. The daughter is like a little mother: always agreeable, pleasant, uncomplaining, and compliant—the representative smiling face with nicely combed hair of the family. The son certainly has a defined role, but as a girl I didn't receive that training. I had a sense that it involved auto repair and being threatening while pretending to tell a joke, but it was shrouded in a sense of mystery.

My father was a sociology professor who taught a class called "Marriage and Family." My family visited this class every year as an expert panel to answer questions about how a family should function. As a child, I enjoyed being an expert, and it was satisfying to know I had official approval for this version of myself.

I came out as bisexual my junior year of high school, which blew a hole through our model family. Throughout my teens and 20s, my parents repeated their dire predictions of what kind of life I would have if I didn't get serious about family formation, as though the nuclear family is as interchangeable and standard as Lego figurines.

As it turned out, my parents loved my partner despite themselves and the fact that she's a woman. They came to our wedding and were loving and supportive through the birth of our first child, a girl.

We found out the baby's presumed sex, which we said was because we wanted to decide on names in advance. I think in truth we were hungry for any information at all about this new little person. We felt tremendous joy that we would get to use the girl name we had treasured for so long, and we had a plan for raising a girl to be strong and independent. We stocked a home library full of stories about independent princesses and famous female scientists, provided a range of clothes and toys from both sections of the store, used evidenced-based parenting strategies, and read through websites such as "A Mighty Girl" to get recommendations for more books, more toys, more ideas to raise this young woman.

The second pregnancy showed Y chromosomes from the baby in my bloodstream. "Congratulations," we were told, "It's a boy!" My reaction to this news was more complicated than I expected; I felt an icy finger of fear cut through the joy. The stakes for raising a boy seemed so high because it would be so easy to get it wrong. What in the world were we supposed to do?

Our son was born in January 2017, the week before the first inauguration of President Donald J. Trump. I watched the inauguration ceremony and saw everything I feared about white masculinity reflected on that stage. I felt the weight of my newborn son curled up in my arms, as light as a feather and as heavy as everything he represented. He was likely to be male, to be tall, to be educated, in fact to be a great deal like the people on that stage with our new president. I turned the TV off when I couldn't take it anymore.

My father was also concerned when he learned we were having a boy, and the veneer of love and acceptance started to chip away. "There will be no father!" he exclaimed. "How does a boy learn how to be a man without a father?!" I understood then what I hadn't growing up: I didn't understand the son role because it was a valuable secret passed down between fathers and sons, men and boys. Women would taint the process. Manhood in this model is a fragile thing.

I strongly disagreed with this belief, and I noted there

were many different ways of being a man and many different types of men. Though I said we would be able to provide a perfectly healthy upbringing for this young person even if he did identify as a boy, inside I wondered whether my father was right. Did we have the tools necessary to raise a son? There's not a burgeoning industry trying to expand the horizons of boys like the girl power phenomenon does for girls. There is no curated library of "Important Kind Men" to read at bedtime and no "A Decent Boy" website to use for gift ideas suitable to the kind and loving male child.

So we make it up as we go along. We question the way society constructs masculinity and places a range of human experiences outside of that, and we try to create space for that expression. We provide dresses and pants, pink and navy, bows and plaid, and we encourage him to choose what he likes. We search for stories about boys who are kind, who work in helping professions, who enjoy the arts, who respect others. And we spend time with adults who identify as men and as feminists to make both of those identities possible.

Every year, it seems to become more socially acceptable to question the traditional boundaries of masculinity. We plan to keep pushing up against them in the hope that this man will have a little more space to breathe.

WALKING WHILE FEMALE: WHAT I WANT MY SON TO KNOW
by Marie Holmes

"Can I take my shirt off too?" my daughter asks.

It's July, and we're on one of the shaded paths in the park, the trees' green leaves dappled with sunlight. She's three years old, and she's watching her seven-year-old brother tear down the hill in his swim trunks, shirtless. We've been creating and destroying water balloons at the playground, the kids slapping them satisfyingly against the fragrant black asphalt faster than I can tie the ends of new ones into knots around my fingers. Usually I have them both in rash guards—pink for her, blue for him, a product of hand-me-downs and, ostensibly, their own preferences. But today Max has been inspired to feel the air on his skin, and Olive wants the same.

I feel a familiar twist in my gut.

107

"Of course!" I say, my smile forced. Olive steps toward me, arms raised in a double salute, and I pull the stretchy fabric over her head. She takes off running after her brother.

♂

I REMEMBER THE MOMENT I became a feminist. I was a girl, a seventh grader, out walking by myself in my suburban neighborhood. I passed through the grounds of my former elementary school, where, in what felt like another lifetime, I had swung on the monkey bars, my shirt dangling uselessly into my face to display the pink coins of my nipples. As I approached the school building that day, a man walked toward me. He was tall and dressed in black, and his long legs quickly brought his body closer and closer to mine. I felt a bubbling in the base of my throat, my pulse skipping. There was no one else around. No one would hear me if I screamed. I walked faster, eyes to the ground as I passed him, then I looked back to make sure he hadn't turned to follow me.

When I reached the sidewalk on the other side of the school, facing a line of pastel bungalows with manicured lawns, my breath began to slow, and I thought, *If I were a boy, nothing about that would've scared me.* I decided right then that I would not live a life circumscribed by fear of rape. My heart thumped solid and fast, my rage raw and righteous.

My son will never know the rush of adrenaline and terror that comes when you realize a man could easily attack you. It isn't that I want him to have this experience, but I want him to know that it exists, to acknowledge it as oppression. I don't want my daughter to experience it either, of course, but I won't get a say in whether she does.

♂

WE HAVEN'T EVEN GOTTEN ALL the way down the hill before Olive's bare chest catches someone's attention. "You're not allowed to go around like *that*," they say to her, though the comment is clearly intended for me. In my memory, the speaker is a man, but they could just as easily have been a woman. *I must look at this person,* I think. *Do I smile?* My reaction was to ignore them.

"What did they say?" asks my son. He understands immediately the unfairness of his being able to go topless while Olive cannot. I tell him it's called a double standard, when things are okay for one group of people but not for another. There are a lot of them for girls, I say.

My daughter wants her shirt back on. My nonchalance hasn't fooled her. She doesn't want that kind of attention, from strangers or from anyone.

In the year that follows, she turns four—big enough to walk a few steps ahead of us. One of the men leaning against the wall of the corner bodega starts saying things. His whole face shifts with a sort of glee. "Blonde!" he exclaims, commenting on her corn-silk-colored hair. He lurches toward her as he goes on about how pretty she is. He is too close.

I watch Olive's tiny face grow quizzical, and as she

casts down her eyes, I see a light in them blink off. Max is there too, taking it all in. He sees me freeze. I stammer. I come to her, but not immediately; not as soon as she needs. "It's okay," I say, although clearly it isn't. "I've got you," I say, meaning, if he touches you, I will fight.

Again, Max has questions. "Why did he scare Olive like that?" I tell him there are men like that everywhere. I should add, *not all men* ... but I don't. I have, mercifully, aged out of cat calls. But the simmering rage is still in me.

"Every time a girl goes out in public," I tell him, "you never know what men are going to say. Sometimes they say disgusting things." He won't have to learn this, the dirty, shameful feeling of knowing just the sight of you has caused someone to think these things. How will he know if I don't tell him that we bear this weight while he is free from it—and with that freedom comes responsibility.

We have to pass the bodega on our way to the train, and Olive starts asking to cross the street to avoid her harasser. Unprompted, Max takes initiative. He runs ahead of us and circles back. "You're safe, Olive, he's not there," he says, then lets us know when we should cross the street. He is learning to shield her, something I hope he continues to do for all the women in his life. Should he have this responsibility as a child, though? Is it frightening for him being the only male in our family?

Max is now 11 and nearly as tall as my wife and me. We all share sweatshirts and shoes, but this is temporary. He will outgrow us. He will be physically capable of protecting us. I hope he never has to use his body to defend us, but I want him to know that he is not helpless to watch harassment take its toll on his sister, nor on every woman he will ever meet. It's a small number of men who do most of the violent harm to women and girls, and as one of their peers he will be in a place to stop some instance of it.

I imagine my son flicking his long blond hair—identical to his sister's—from his face, saying, "Dude, that's fucked up. Don't say that." My heart swells with anticipatory pride.

INTERVIEW: ELLIOTT O. WRIGHT AND KATE OKESON
by Ada Malone

Elliott Wright is a 19-year-old student at Rutgers University who spent most of his life raised by his mother, Kate Okeson. Elliott identifies as "a straight white guy," and Kate describes herself as *not* "a gold star gay," though she's been queer her whole life. Kate was with Elliott's father until Elliott was three, and she is twice divorced. While she has had several partners throughout Elliott's life, she says, "Elliott and I sort of always had our own kind of separate thing. We were pretty aligned in our own way ... We made our own way."

Kate and Elliott both see "friends as family" as an important philosophical choice. As Kate puts it, "Elliott grew up around folks that were adults he could rely on, that he could talk to, that were invited into a family space. And part of that was also my decision around developing

113

positive relationships with adults. You know ... choosing who is your family, modeling that, choosing who you want to spend your time with. He didn't have to be dragged along to yet another terrible holiday."

Elliott agrees with his mother's description of their small nuclear family and extended chosen family, adding that he feels the "model of chosen family" is something his mother "passed on" to him. "Our family unit is kind of just the people we surround ourselves with," he says. He describes their Christmas dinners as family dinners, but with more friends than family. They also moved the tradition to Boxing Day because many people couldn't make it on Christmas, but it's still a "stable tradition." Kate adds, "Elliott's dad is part of the community. He's Elliott's family, and he's by extension my family still, too. The world's already hard enough—we need people we can count on no matter what."

Kate and Elliott live in a community that has some folks who hold "some pretty rigid views about gender and marriage, pretty heteronormative, driven by a culture of machismo." Because of that, there were some incidents early on in Elliott's life—during first and second grades— when there was a lot of judgment and some "crazy epithets" that needed to be addressed. As Kate explains, "But the conversation at home was not like, 'These are bad words.' It was more in the context of our family: 'This is actually even more significant or more hurtful.'"

While the culture of their community says, "Well, kids aren't old enough to talk about X, Y, or Z," Kate never took that approach with Elliott. Early on, she discussed with him the language around "consent, around personal space, around affirmation, acceptance even. And as he [acquired] language, some of those conversations through time [became], 'Just because somebody says, "Boys don't do that" doesn't mean we actually hold that belief.' There's a lot of continual talking about and unpacking of gender roles."

Kate goes on to describe the assumptions made by folks in the community they live in, especially when Elliott was younger. In a grocery store once, they ran into a child Elliott knew who asked, "Is that your aunt or your uncle?" Kate notes, "I was both misgendered and [seen as] not possibly his [immediate] family member." At other times, community members would doubt that Kate could be Elliot's parent and ask things like, "Oh, where's his mother?" Kate says that addressing these assumptions in an open way at home with her son was the norm. "We always talked out loud about what it felt like to run into other people's assumptions."

Elliott expresses that for him, as a six, seven, and eight-year-old kid, he didn't really think twice about the gender of the person his mom was dating; however, the outside world would come crashing in, and he felt confused by that intrusion. "It was never a question of my mom's dating a woman but more so that we'd encounter things [like] people using really hurtful language or making assumptions. [Both] were hurtful and didn't make sense to me as a [child]."

Thankfully, Kate found one of her "first best allies" in Elliott's first grade teacher after an incident on the bus when Elliott was called the F-slur for wearing nail polish. While Elliott had never heard that word before, he knew it was bad (as kids always do). Initially, Kate was clued in that something was wrong when Elliott came home wanting to remove the nail polish but didn't want to talk about it. Then, as kids so often do in the quiet intimacy of bedtime when their minds and bodies are tired and unable to fight back the feelings and emotions, Elliott finally did share with his mom the word he had been called. "And this is first grade. Right? I'm like, How do kids even know what this is?" Kate pondered. "I was like, 'Well, that must not have felt very good,' and we talked a lot about his feelings first. I remember telling him, 'I need to think about this [be]cause … as much as it hurt you, it also hurts me, and I'm not sure how I want to respond yet.'" Ultimately, after talking through Elliott's feelings, she left it up to him what he wanted to do about wearing or removing the nail polish. "It was all his choice."

Kate softens a bit as she provides a cultural perspective to the behavior the other kids exhibited toward Elliott. The elementary school Elliott attended had a majority Latinx population with less than 10 percent of the students being white. Most of the kids attending were "navigating a couple of languages on a regular basis— stuff like that. And there [was] a real strong gendered culture. Some of that [was] also embedded in the faith approaches of these families, and it also made it hard for Elliott to have friends." Because of these incidents, what became very intentional in Kate's parenting was having conversations with Elliott "around understanding that I walk the world a little differently than maybe some of his other friends' parents."

Conversations about privilege were also common in

their household while Elliott was growing up. In fact, Elliott credits those conversations to his decision to study political science. Kate describes the time that a childhood friend of hers, Dennis, a Black man, was over for dinner. They were discussing upcoming Supreme Court cases, and Dennis turned to Elliott and said, "Well, of the three of us at this table, who has the most privilege here?" His point was that none of those cases appearing before the Supreme Court were going to take away any of Elliott's privileges. Later, Elliott admitted to his mom that he "was not interested in feeling like that right now." It was a lot for him to carry, yet now, as he pursues his degree, he reflects, "I'm in a very unique position in that if the government does anything privilege-wise, I won't be affected. But everyone I care about will be."

When asked if he's a feminist, Elliott's short answer is yes, but as he thoughtfully points out, he had a lot to think through to get to that answer. As with so many things, he figured it out through conversations with his mom. As "a straight white guy," Elliott sees himself as "the enemy ... the image of the patriarchy." Through talking this over with Kate, though, he came around to see that "I could be an ally. But like, I know a lot of fake allies," and he doesn't want to be like that.

Kate and Elliott go on to explain that language choice, especially how they spoke about other people, was especially important in their household. They recall a story when Kate's parents were watching Elliott, and her dad, while reading the paper with Elliott, "demonized" Hilary Clinton. Kate told her mom, "I love you and I love Dad, but I can love you both at a distance, and we're not going to do this. We don't talk about people that way." Elliott regularly saw Kate openly but kindly speak out against "cultural microaggression-y misogyny. He had a sense of like, "We don't say X, Y, and Z about people. But I really spent time trying to say, 'That comment's not designed to be an inclusive statement,' 'This comment is meant to undermine or do that,' or 'That's about gaslighting people, and that's gendered.' I spent a lot of time pointing these things out because we are always working across difference; we're always communicating across difference. And you need to have a well-adapted honed lens to see all of that."

Feelings were normalized in Kate and Elliott's household. "The whole thing was like, 'It's okay to have feelings.' My mom was always like, 'One, you gotta feel your feelings, and two, feelings are normal.' So it's like normalizing being able to be a full-fledged human being. And I definitely know some people who didn't have that. They were like, 'A man shouldn't feel these feelings,' that type of stuff. I'm very lucky to have grown up in an environment where that wasn't the case. I feel like I'm particularly well-versed in talking about my feelings."

As the interview draws to a close, we discuss ideas around identity and nature versus nurture. Elliott describes how he was frequently misgendered as a child and it upset him a lot. "I didn't really understand why, other than I wanted to be recognized as who I was." As he got older, he says, this was no longer an issue for him, as he's surrounded by peers now at college who are genderqueer or on the spectrums of sexuality and/or gender. Elliott knows, though, that what was an easy, open conversation in his home isn't always so for his peers who are in the process of exploring their own identities.

For her part, Kate takes great pride in Elliott's level of awareness around these issues. "[There's] almost nothing more powerful in the world than to raise somebody who's a young man who will choose and maintain a philosophy of anti-racism, feminism, and affirming of people's identities."

THE SALAD SPINNER CHRONICLES
by Gail Marlene Schwartz

Lately, my formerly mellow baby boy has turned into a maniacally obsessive student of domestic life in our Montreal home. Considering his prior preoccupation with trucks, I'm guessing his developing character is flexing its yin muscles to, however clumsily, attempt balance. I should be overjoyed, but frankly I find it more than a little disturbing.

The first indication showed itself one day while I was baking muffins. I wish I could say "while I was repairing the leaky toilet" or "while I was putting in a new tiled backsplash," but that would be taking more than my fair share of artistic license. Alexi was rummaging through the Tupperware cabinet in the kitchen, the one kitchen cabinet my wife Lucie and I allow him to explore. I turned my back to grab the brown sugar when I heard a crash behind me. The three distinct parts of our beloved salad spinner tumbled across the bathwater-gray kitchen floor. Then I heard a throaty cry that seemed to bubble up from my boy's innards and explode from his gaping mouth. But his expression was not distress; it was a scream of sheer delight and discovery. I looked at him, confused, and then picked up the plastic colander-like bowl.

"*This?*" I said to him with disbelief. "This is what you want?"

He smiled, pointed, and said, "Babawawa."

Since this was Quebec and we never watched the program *20/20*, I knew he didn't mean Barbara Walters. Something about the salad spinner had attracted his attention, and it was clear he wanted me to deliver it intact. Always open to new ideas, I put the three pieces together and placed boy and spinner in a gated play area.

Pure joy ensued.

For a good two months, the salad spinner fully occupied my son's leisure time. He never tired of pumping the spin mechanism, staring at the middle piece whizzing around, listening with fascination to plastic hitting plastic, pushing the black button that stops the action, and getting any adult with a free finger to click the white latch that locks the middle piece in place. Nothing, not a new-to-him drum, a Caillou plastic bath book, or even a walking talking programmable robot could woo him away from his new favorite toy.

Nothing, that was, until he discovered the vacuum cleaner.

Our wonderful babysitter, Megan, spent a few hours a week vacuuming the house. Maybe it was sleep deprivation, but I could swear she had been doing it the exact same way since Alexi came home from the hospital. Yet one day the vacuum was part of the invisible white noise of the household, and the next day it was a baby Saab. I admit that Lucie and I splurged a bit on this item, and perhaps there are adults who would find our yellow Miele super-efficient, or even, possibly, sleek. But to Alexi, discovering the Miele was like being born again. Thank goodness this second time did not involve my uterus.

Lucie, Megan, and I tried not to laugh at Alexi's expressions of ardor, and Megan even let him help push it across the living room carpet on occasion. The problem came when the floors were clean and it was time for the Miele to go back into the front hall closet. Alexi, who had just once in his 13 months shown a preference for any toy, began howling like a car door had closed on his finger (don't ask me how I know what this sounds like). Trying to console him proved useless for a good 10 minutes. He was grieving.

Last week I had a day-long training in Vermont, the longest time that Alexi and I have ever been separated. I called every night to see how things were going and to say hi to my kiddo. One night, when Lucie answered the phone, her French accent seemed stronger.

"I drank half a glass of wine," she admitted. I asked her what had happened, trying to stay calm.

"It was endless, just endless. First, he fell on the sidewalk when we took the dog this morning and got a big egg on his forehead. Once we recovered from that, and without you it's longer—"

"Without my breasts, you mean," I interrupted.

"He dropped Petey on the way home, and this Irish Setter came out of nowhere and grabbed it and dashed off. No more Petey."

I groaned. I wondered briefly if I could find another Petey the stuffed seahorse online before remembering we had gotten him at a garage sale.

"Then we went to call you, and the cell phone was dead, and I couldn't find the charger. At one point in the afternoon, he finally had enough."

"Was this when you had the glass of wine?"

She ignored me. "I was trying to calm him down after bath time, but he just kept crying and crying. So I went into the front hall closet to get the baby carrier to wear him in. I opened the door, and before I even laid eyes on the sling, our boy had thrown his arms around the vacuum cleaner."

I cracked up and quickly crossed my legs, praying the Kegels had done their magic.

"He cuddled up to the thing and sighed," she went on. "He stayed in the closet, clinging to the Miele for twenty minutes. Then he was done, and with a little hiccup he turned to me and took my hand, and we went up to bed."

When I got home from Vermont, we decided we needed Alexi to take some distance from the Miele so we could resume our regular housecleaning routine. We did what many 21st century parents would do: We looked for a toy substitute. Incredibly, Lucie found one in perfect condition for $2 at the local Goodwill. It was brightly colored, toddler-sized, and had a noise that truly mimicked the sucking mechanism of a vacuum. He loved it, played with it even more than the salad spinner, and gave it kisses when that loving feeling overwhelmed him.

But unfortunately, he couldn't break things off with the Miele. His obsession with the real deal continued, and Lucie and I found ourselves speaking about the vacuum in code, sneaking it out of the closet when he was outside, and hiding it behind doors, under my writer's desk, and even once in the shower.

This got old, fast.

I decided to go with the flow, save energy, and build some arm strength: I brought out my old broom and dustpan. Unfortunately, just this week, he was showing the same tendencies toward these more primitive tools. I tried to lure him away with his yellow Tonka bulldozer, his favorite book about caterpillars, and his riding toddler bus, but to no avail. I tried my best not to roll my eyes when he asked, yet again, to go get the blue broom and sweep the back porch.

I tell myself I should be happy my little boy is finding work associated with women so fascinating. I tell myself how great it is that he is learning these very practical skills and that he will even be able to do some of these jobs himself soon. I tell myself this might be an advantage of growing up as a boy with two queer moms: There is nobody to react negatively to these early passions. And I tell myself that this kind of obsessiveness is necessary to become truly great at anything.

All these things I know to be true. My problem is that I can't think of anything duller than those very domestic chores he is currently gaga over. I would rather spend the day watching a cement foundation get poured than repeatedly sweeping, vacuuming, or spinning salad. It's bad enough I have to do those chores myself as necessary adult tasks, but to do them ad nauseam with an edgy toddler is not my idea of fun.

When I'm in a more pensive mood, I think that perhaps another gift our children bring us is a fresh look at daily activities we take for granted as tedious. Maybe I should change my approach to being frustrated or down. Perhaps if I sat in the middle of the floor and explored the joys of my salad spinner on a bad day, I would not only feel better but possibly change my attitude toward housework. Who knows? Maybe the mental and emotional benefits of spinning salad will be my next post that goes viral on social media.

ONE FAMILY'S JOURNEY EXPLORING EMOTIONAL SENSITIVITY
by Brie Radis

My oldest child, Asher, was sitting in the middle of the playground sobbing hysterically. He ran to me and nuzzled into the crook of my neck, breathing deeply and gasping in deep gulps of air. He explained that a friend had said he couldn't join in their game, and it had really hurt his feelings. We talked, and I comforted him by listening and giving him another hug. At almost nine years old, my son was not yet embarrassed about displaying emotions or revealing his heartbreak in public settings.

Asher has always been an emotionally sensitive and expressive child. During suspenseful Marvel or *Star Wars* movies (that his peers have rewatched with little noticeable alarm), Asher would cover his eyes or run out of the room in an attempt to escape from the tension and uncertainty. He was also an avid reader of a range of fantasy, mystery, and action-oriented novels and would read them over and over, which allowed him to pace his experience. Now that he is a tween, he is often overwhelmed by the portrayal of personal moments when someone is experiencing tenderness, shame, or fear. During these cinematic moments, Asher leaves the room overwhelmed, and he does not return until the emotional interaction is over. His early responses to strong feelings of fear around danger and violence have transformed to include empathy for characters who are distraught or worried.

Our society continues to struggle with the economic, political, and social expectations that accompany patriarchy and gender roles and expectations for boys and men (Rosen and Nofziger 2019). Traditional gender roles perpetuated by the cultural archetype of the American masculine ideal embolden the stereotype of the strong, confident boy who is expected to follow the mantra "Boys will be boys" (Ford 2019). Through constant messaging, a toxic masculinity emerges that glorifies strength, virility, and dominance (Rogers et al. 2019). This masculinity also suppresses vulnerable emotions and encourages the use of aggression and violence to solve problems and assert power.

As feminist-identified parents, my wife and I strive to affirm and empower our son's strengths and encourage growth in his empathy and communication as we join with others who are rethinking stereotypical masculinity. My wife and I fell in love in college and spent a decade child free before choosing the same willing-to-be-known donor for both of our children. I gave birth to Asher, and two and half years later my wife gave birth to our younger child, who identifies as nonbinary. To protect our family, we both did a second parent adoption through the local court system for the child that we did not give birth to. My partner and I started our relationship prioritizing the use of emotional language and have continued this pattern of expression with both of our children following queer, feminist, and anti-oppression-based value systems. When our children were infants, we encouraged them to use nonverbal sign language to communicate their feelings. Asher followed suit by developing an advanced language around emotions and comfort when discussing challenging topics. We freely talk about emotions and our mental well-being on long car trips, during bedtime rituals, and at the dinner table.

When Asher entered first grade, where the kids were around six years old, we noticed that some of his close friends and his teammates from sports were becoming less and less comfortable discussing feelings or responding to Asher's outward expressions of emotion. We often found ourselves feeling hurt or worried and even doubting ourselves as parents when others were outwardly judgmental about Asher's emotions. Some adult friends and even family members offered negative comments, blaming his behavior on us. Although he has heard the classic toxic admonishments and taunts such as "Big boys don't cry," Asher continues to feel and express a range of emotions including sadness and joy as well as anger, but he is becoming increasingly aware of how others are perceiving him.

My partner and I have discussed how we may have been too encouraging about sharing emotions. We questioned the need to guide our son to express feelings in a safe, more private space and manner. We wanted to protect our child from harmful feedback from others but also provide him with helpful tools and skills needed to navigate a culture that is negative toward boys' expression of vulnerable emotions. To support Asher, we committed to family therapy and began talking to him about containment and safe times to express his strong feelings. We said things like, "Your feelings are very important and a safe place to express these feelings is at home with your moms" and "If you feel yourself become overwhelmed by a situation or with another person, it's important to pause and reflect and figure out the next thing you can do in this situation." Tender masculinity provides a framework that we use to encourage self-awareness, comfort with expressing emotions freely, and ways to embrace emotional intimacy in relationships and have healthy boundaries in our family. We also recognize the privilege around our queer family being white and middle class; due to white supremacy, there is more space and societal acceptance in expressing feelings when compared to queer parents and caregivers from other racial groups.

While many are not comfortable with emotions, using a template such as the Mad, Sad, Glad retrospective has been helpful to our family as we check on our emotional well-being. Exploring Asher's feelings of frustration or annoyance (mad), disappointment (sad), and what has made him feel happy or proud (glad) is helping him develop a stronger set of behaviors and language. He is learning to focus on the discussion of events, behaviors, and actions as opposed to blaming or aggressive problem-solving. Becoming more self-aware and learning to explore why he might be upset or what makes him feel especially angry or sad are additional areas of growth for Asher. He has identified that the lack of equity or feeling left out in a situation are areas he is aware of, and he is experimenting with this awareness in his relationships.

As our now 11-year-old grows, we are determined he will not be in that 23% of young men who believe that males need to use violence and aggression to earn respect, as reported in *The Man Box* (Heilman et al. 2017). We are hopeful he continues to practice expressing himself in safe ways while maintaining his emotional well-being and identity.

Now when Asher is struggling with a relationship, such as a recent conflict with a close friend or his sibling, we often explore with him ways to manage his time, space, and boundaries. He has learned to verbalize his preferences clearly and has developed the ability to talk about a disagreement in a calmer state of mind, which fosters emotional balance while avoiding the ever-present trap of toxic masculinity.

GINGERBREAD PERSONS AND STAYING OUT OF OUR KIDS' WAY: INTERVIEW WITH MEADOW AND JENN BRAUN

by Ada Malone

Meadow and Jenn Braun are moms to a set of boy/girl twins, Indra and Eko. Indra was assigned male at birth and currently identifies as such. The family explained that they identify as racially and ethnically mixed Afro-Euro-Asian-Jewish. Meadow, the bio-mom, says she is Afro/Jewish and Jenn says she is Indonesian-Dutch/Euro. The children's donor is Euro/Chinese, making the children a mix of Afro/Jewish/Euro/Chinese, and, Jenn adds, culturally they are also Indonesian-Dutch, as they are raised with her traditions as well. For example, their favorite meal is an Indonesian dish

Jenn prepares called "Oma Sophie's Hot Coconut Chicken." This diverse range of racial and cultural influences shapes their family, giving Indra an implied understanding that he "comes from different types of people in different parts of the world."

In some ways, Meadow and Jenn note during our interview, race and ethnicity "may be bigger for us in a way than gender awareness." But, as they point out, like many of the boys in this collection, there's no escaping the fact that Indra is living in a house full of women and thus "surrounded by female energy."

Having twins of different genders provides a unique perspective when it comes to parenting choices they make with the intention of supporting the development of healthy masculinity in their son. For Jenn and Meadow, this idea of feminist parenting is inextricable from the fact that their children are boy/girl "counterparts" or "mirrors" of each other, as they describe it. "I think their lives are so different because of the dynamic of each other," Meadow says. "[Eko is] seeing a boy that's sort of like this mirror of her all the time, and [Indra is] seeing a girl, so I think that that's actually really special for them."

Jenn and Meadow are frequently thinking about how they treat Indra in comparison to Eko, and because of this, issues of gender are on their minds perhaps even more often than they are for those of us raising only sons. As Meadow puts it, "You're constantly faced with this gender question all along because of that. Like, *Am I doing this differently because this is a boy and this is a girl? Am I not doing it differently? Should I [be]?* You're constantly asking [those] question[s] all the time when it comes to your responses to their behavior, to their clothing."

Continuing, they describe frequently thinking about their actions after having treated Indra a certain way, questioning whether they would have treated Eko the same. Meadow says, "Sometimes I noticed myself maybe responding to him in a way that I worry is harsher than the way I might be responding to her; even if it's not, I have to ask myself the question, Am I responding to him different[ly] than I would to her in a similar circumstance?"

Jenn is quick to agree: "Yeah, I definitely do the same. I always try to think, *Would I do this with Eko?* Or if he's being dramatic or crying, I'm careful about saying, 'Oh, you're okay' or 'Don't cry, it's okay.' I try to just let him do it, but I'm consciously thinking about that ... like, *Okay, if he's feeling emotional about it, just let him be emotional.*"

Meadow admits to sometimes "responding to him in a way that I worry is harsher ... And so, then I have to kind of stop myself and say, *How would I respond if it [were] Eko?* and then try to make that my response [to] him."

The challenge with this though, they point out, is that Indra and Eko "have very different personalities." So in moments when they're trying to parent consciously from the perspective of gender, trying to ensure fairness and equity despite gender differences, they are also faced with the same issue all parents are faced with: Kids have separate characters, and at times we need to measure our responses to our children based on who they are as people, not based on their gender.

The topic of gender, however, looms large in all our lives. When I ask them if they notice "gendered" differences between their kids, I have to quickly clarify: "By gendered, I mean attributes that we typically assign to each gender."

They speak almost simultaneously in asserting, "Yes. Definitely."

I then ask, "How would you characterize that?"

Meadow shares a story: "I have a friend with twins who are a few years older, who talked to me about this when ours were babies and hers were probably a little younger. She was saying how it's shocking to her how gendered the twins are even though they tried so hard not to [parent that way]. You're living in this world, and it's very hard to not let those things seep in. Impossible. But now seeing them grow up, I also think they just come into the world a certain way."

When describing those gendered differences between their own kids, Meadow goes on to say, "In terms of the very stereotypical kind of gender stuff, he's more straight-forward. He's more physical, more rough-and-tumble. He's less aware of his body in a way, like he throws himself around."

Jenn adds, "I'll notice moments with him, like over the years, where he just needs to be physical, to wrestle or throw a pillow, and I just do that with him. He just needs it, you know, whereas Eko is like, 'Don't do it!'" She then recalls, "I've always said, since he was like a baby, I remember … describing him as sincere, which is very sweet, but also in the sense that he doesn't hide anything about the way he feels. He's just very straightforward, there's no mystery." With Eko, on the other hand, "It's like, 'What's going on?' [There are] layers and layers of complexity with her communication."

Meadow adds, "Oh, and then also he walked sooner than her but talked later."

In general, Meadow and Jenn describe developmental attributes that are frequently attributed to each gender—things like "boys talk later"—which they saw play out with their twins. Meadow recalls that when Eko and Indra were around the ages of 16–18 months, "I was walking around feeling like I basically had a little sidekick I was communicating with all day, Eko … like I was fully having conversations with her, and [Indra] was like, 'What?' He was like a baby."

Both Jenn and Meadow tend to agree that while they watched their two children grow up, they could see gendered stereotypes as having some amount of validity, stating that Indra was "very much stereotypically boy" and that "it does not seem like we created that." However, they were quick to add, "It's hard because you just don't want to assign everything to gender. You don't want to think everything is just about gender, because he's also a different kid. He has some sensory stuff that [Eko] just doesn't have. He's very specific about textures and foods, and she'll eat anything. But that's just who he is, and I mean a lot of that has nothing to do with gender."

We go on to discuss the ways in which our views about gender as constructed come up against the realities of raising a human in our homes who is simply different from us in many ways, and many of those are in stereotypically gendered ways. The primary difference we keep coming back to is simply the apparent "need" to be physically assertive in ways that we as moms don't necessarily relate to. My son Levi, for instance, loves to wrestle, do karate chops, and throw punches. These are all things I cannot stand to do, see, or experience. I send my wife, who is much more masculine than I am, to do those things with him, but even for her this kind of physicality doesn't seem to come naturally.

Meadow and Jenn describe that for the first three years of the twins' lives, they felt that their "full time job was basically to protect [Eko] from being physically harmed ... It was insane. It was so scary because [Indra was] just all over her. He [was] a bulldozer. So yeah, he's a bulldozer and she's not. That's just how they are."

At this point during the interview, they reiterate that this kind of more aggressive behavior was not something they encouraged. They set themselves apart from parents who have their newborns in a "little slugger onesie" and push their young baby boys to behave in ways deemed "manly." Their approach, in fact, was quite the opposite. Jenn said, "A word I said to Indra a lot in the beginning was 'gentle.'"

As Indra has gotten older, that gentleness has also revealed itself. They describe him as "Full-on. So if it's rough, it's rough, but if it's something else ... he's super sensitive and super loving, and he wants to come up and rub his nose on you and give kisses. He's always giving us kisses. He can be the sweetest, softest, most gentle little person."

When asked whether they have any moments they would define as a failure at feminist parenting, Meadow lightly says, "I don't think we're yet at the point of failure. I think the jury's still out on the job we're doing. So we haven't failed yet, but I definitely have times where I'm like, *Oh God, have we messed that up already?*" They both agree this comes up most often when Indra says that a girl cannot do a certain thing. "And you just realize," says Meadow, "it's not so much that we did something that failed, but you feel a little bit like, *Did we fail at [being] clear or being vocal enough? Maybe we should have sheltered them more from certain things so that that message didn't get through*—like somehow it seeps through."

At this point, Meadow pauses.

She goes on. "Maybe just by virtue of living in this culture and having grown up in this culture, we have somehow let that message come through in the way we joke around about something, in our tone, [in] the language we use about certain things, or [with] what we choose to watch or not watch. I mean, they just get all the little subtleties."

In situations when Indra expresses doubt about a girl's ability to do something, Jenn and Meadow have a quick counterargument that not all parents can go to: They'll ask Indra, "Do you think Eko can't do this? And would you like it if someone said this about Eko?" Quick to come to his twin sister's defense, Indra quickly responds with the realization that he would not like that at all, and he will affirm his belief that "Eko can do anything."

Jenn and Meadow also noted moments of feminist parenting success when Indra has returned their own lesson to them. Meadow was once talking about sports and referenced a sportsman, and Indra quickly corrected her with, "or sportswoman." And with our interview being around the holidays, Meadow notes having to say "gingerbread person" around 20 times in the days prior, as Indra was intent on reminding everyone to talk about their gingerbread people in gender-neutral ways.

Another time they were made to live their own lessons was when Indra wanted to wear a dress to school. Throughout the pandemic, he'd been wearing dresses at home for virtual school to match his twin sister. But the first time he wanted to attend in-person school wearing a dress, Jenn admits to catching her breath. "I was nervous for him," she said, "for what kids would say or how a teacher might react or whatever ... But ... you have to just let them be, and he was fine. He navigated it. He said, 'Some people asked me why I was wearing a dress, [and I told them it was] because it's fashion.' He had his little sayings, and he was able to navigate it."

Making conscious choices about gender pronoun usage has also been important to Jenn and Meadow in raising both of their children. Meadow consciously chooses to use "she" at least 50 percent of the time "about all the random things. So if I see an animal in the yard, it's 'she.' She. She. Sometimes I'm like, *I'm saying it too much*, but then I'm like, *No, you can't possibly say it too much—even if I say it 100 percent of the time*." Similarly, when the kids were little and couldn't read, Jenn and Meadow would change the gender pronouns in all of the anthropomorphized characters (such as in *Little Blue Truck* and *Goodnight, Goodnight, Construction Site*). They "wanted to somehow diversify what they heard as much as possible in the early years while we felt like we had some control."

As we begin discussing the fact that the kids can now

read and will one day discover that these books don't use the "she" pronoun, Meadow starts to express concern that we aren't actually changing anything by making these minor interventions. But in the end, she decided, "We're raising the question. I mean, we're not going to pretend the world is different from what it is, but at some point we begin to have conversations about how the world actually is and why we disagree. And they'll have the basis that we've [been planting] all along."

The Brauns' advice for all parents, regardless of who they are parenting, is this: "Just let them be themselves. Don't see what they're doing and then say, 'Hmm I don't know if I quite like that. Let me try to nudge that more toward what I think is acceptable.' ... You want to just be able to express yourself and be who you are and not feel ashamed of how you're acting, how you're being, or what you're becoming."

With Indra, their guidepost to raising a son with a healthy relationship to gender means just allowing "him to feel that it's okay to be the person he is, whatever that is. Some of it's going to fit into a masculinity kind of bubble, and some of it won't, and all of that is cool."

It all boils down to "Just let your children be. Let them be," says Meadow.

Jenn is quick to add, "And don't bring your own shit into it."

TIME TO CHANGE THE CHANNEL
by Lalita du Perron

There is a common misconception that boys growing up in a household with a lesbian feminist mom will naturally be feminist and progressive. I guess I labored under that misconception too. My son's conception was a misconception in so many ways, as it did not involve sex, an expectation of a traditional family, or even a second parent. Labor is a whole other story. After the man-free misconception, I wanted a patriarchy-free labor. No OB/GYN, no wires, no numbers, no drugs. The only man present at my son's birth was him, but I did not know that at the time—I had fought off the cultural expectation of finding out my baby's sex in utero. After he surfed out into the birthing pool I had installed in my apartment, I stared at him in amazement, primarily delighted that the mind-numbing pain of labor was over. It must have been only 10 seconds, but it felt much longer before my doula said, "It's a boy."

As a single mother by choice, I deeply felt the enormous responsibility of raising a boy in the patriarchy we live in. From the get-go I had an open-door bathroom policy. Surely there is no easier way for a boy to be comfortable around female body stuff than watching his mom sort out a sanitary pad.

"Does it hurt?" he asked the first time he understood what blood meant, when he was three or four years old.

"Not really," I replied. "But I do get a little grouchy. It hurts my head more than it does my body."

A few months later, when I was yelling at him for something inconsequential (does anyone ever yell about something that is actually important?), he asked me sweetly and innocently, "Are you having your period, Mom?"

How to explain that yes, that is a compassionate way of trying to understand a woman's unpredictable mood swings, but no, that is not a question that should *ever* be asked?

As part of my queer vision, I tried to educate my son with consequences, not punishment. I'd tell him that there is no supreme male being who sits in judgment of you, but if you do X, Y will naturally happen. One day when my son was around six, we were listening to the radio in the car, and an Eminem song came on. I changed the channel.

"Why don't we listen to that singer, Mom?" came the question from the backseat.

"Because he beat up his wife," I explained.

Silence ensued, during which I imagined my son was

146

reflecting on the evils of domestic violence.

Then the question, "But what did she do?"

My son, I think. *When I put you in time out as a consequence for a misbehavior, I tell you, "I love you, but that is not acceptable behavior. You are a good person, but what you did was not good."*

Being versus doing. Actions have reactions. Behavior has consequences. But when a fully grown man beats up his wife, that is not a consequence. She did nothing to warrant that, and he is not a good boy who made a bad decision. He is an a-hole.

So, we are changing the channel. But is my teenage son able to change his internalized channel of which actions deserve reactions and which require judgment?

I don't know when my son first understood what sex actually is, because the first years of his life when he would ask about it, I would give him such a lengthy preamble about consent that he would lose interest by the time I could get to anything graphic about people's bodies. Once, when we were on a bus with a group of under-graduates with whom I was working, a female student shared a story about her mom telling her that babies were conceived by two people "having a special hug."

"That's weird," said my son, all of ten years old. "Why would she not just tell you about sex?"

The students expressed admiration: "You have such a cool mom!"

My son shrugged that off. "Nah. She just told me some parents have sex to have a baby. Others, like her, go to a clinic." He then went back to reading his book, much more interesting than young adult chatter.

My son, a teenager now, knows women are strong,

financially independent, and in charge. He knows gender is a construct, people use different pronouns, there aren't boy things and girl things, and all the things we assume a boy raised in a lesbian feminist household would know and think. And yet, the antiestablishment context of his upbringing notwithstanding, my son is a (self-declared) straight white male living in a world that has people who look like him at its front and center. He lives in a universe that pushes back against my influence at every turn. From being asked in school to write an essay about "my dad" for Father's Day to being told that as a boy he could not wear nail polish and hearing "gay" used as a slur, he sees white heteropatriarchal supremacy in all its forms in action every single day.

It dawned on me not that long ago that my son has grown up never seeing a man doing anything we would traditionally classify as female work. So yes, he knows women can top up their engine oil and check their tire pressure. But he also knows women cook, clean, volunteer, and other things I would like him not to expect women to do. His daily chores are not going to mitigate the messages he receives from the world we inhabit and to which I have no doubt also contributed.

My son once walked in on me when I was shaving my legs. "Why are you doing that?" he asked.

"Because I like my legs to be without hair," I replied, frantically trying to think of smart feminist things to say and wishing I had for once locked the bathroom door. "But that doesn't mean body hair isn't beautiful. Some women love having hairy legs. Others, like your mom, not so much."

Who knows what he took away from that conversation? Maybe that moms are complex beings. Maybe that it's human to be contradictory. Maybe that women make up their own beauty standards. I just hope he forgets that my razor was pink.

SOAPBOX
by Ada Malone

On family walks and while peering out our sliding glass doors into the backyard, we commonly see creatures hop, bound, fly, or slide by. Too often (almost always), my wife and I default to using "he" as we point and exclaim things like, "Look at the bird! Did you see him?" Our son, Levi, will respond with, "How do you know it's a boy or a girl?" After all, we haven't examined its markings nor its genitalia. Likewise, he will often ask this same question when we label a human that we don't know as a specific gender. In these situations, my wife and I have our lessons about gender fluidity handed back to us and are reminded that not assuming another person's (or animal's) gender is an important concept in our family.

As my wife and I falter on our own teaching, we notice how difficult it is to keep this knowledge of gender fluidity at the forefront of our thinking when we've been culturally programmed for decades to think of gender in binary terms and to use "he" as a pronoun for everyone (and everything). We also recognize how much we stand to learn from our own kiddo as long as we keep trying hard to teach him these concepts around gender that might run counter to what he experiences daily outside our home.

"There is no gender," Levi will say. While we work hard to make sure he is aware that ideas about items being for a specific gender are mere constructs, I don't actually believe that there is "no gender." But this is how Levi has internalized all the times I've told him there are no girl colors and no boy colors, no girl clothes and no boy clothes, no girl toys and no boy toys. Sure, there are colors, clothes, and toys marketed to a specific gender, but in the end, I tell him, this is all about capitalism and constructed beliefs about gender. Play with any toy you want. Wear any color you like. Gender is a construct, I tell him often.

My approach is a bit didactic, I suppose. Yet I know of no other way to fight the ridiculousness around gender stereotypes other than to outright say they are not grounded in anything other than human imagination.

Levi lives in a two-mom household where women's issues cannot be avoided. He hears about periods and hot flashes, he sees bras blowing in the wind on the clothesline, and he hears a lot about hormones and their effects on mood and overall bodily feeling. He simply witnesses the everyday lives of women. This acts as a quiet complement to all my lectures and passionate social justice rants about cultural gender misconceptions.

He also sees my wife, his Didi, as strong as any man. There isn't anything we cannot do here simply because there are no men involved. We haul wood and bags of concrete. We build decks, forts, and swing sets. We play sports with him during the day, and at night he stitches embroidery with me as we rock in the same glider where I held him daily to my breast. I cook dinner and then we build Lego. We watch TV shows and comment on their inclusivity, but we also read books with female superheroes and treat it as not even worth noting.

At night, Levi and I crawl into his dinosaur-clad bed, excited to read as we plow through the Ramona Quimby series. He giggles with delight when Ramona is obstinate—when she rides her tricycle into Beezus and Henry's game of checkers and when she leaves her rain boots in a mud puddle, arriving to her classroom wet and sock-footed. When Levi asks his friends whether they read Ramona, they wrinkle their faces in confusion. I tense up, worrying he'll be made fun of for reading "girly" books. Most of them have never heard of her. When the other parents ask what we are reading and I tell them the Ramona Quimby books, they pause, searching their memories. One of the moms remembers loving those books as a kid, and a few of the dads nod in vague recollection, but their kids are reading about Harry Potter and Percy Jackson.

While I don't want Levi to be left out of Percy Jackson's odyssey, it seems to be dominated by Zeus's master bolt and his brother Poseidon's big spear. Weapons and violence. Kronos and his army preparing for battle. Sure, there is Thalia, as well as Artemis with her eternal virginity. But the covers are filled with explosions, fire, shirtless gods, and a creepy cyclops. Levi is six years old. He is highly entertained by and adores Ramona. He loves Pippi Longstocking too; he admires her ability to survive on her own, outsmart crooks, and hoist men and horses above her head. He loves female characters that are audacious and strong and go against the grain. I intend to nurture this love for as long as I can.

Some other things Levi has said are "Boys can't marry boys" and "Two girls cannot kiss." Recently he has discovered the word "gay" being used—not in the way we use it in this house to mean either happy or attracted to people of one's own gender, but in the way it gets spit out furiously on the school yard and in quiet classroom huddles safe from the teacher's ears. When he says these things, I counter them aggressively, saying, "That is simply not true. What about your moms? They are girls, and they kiss. Where did you hear this from?" Inevitably, it came from one of his friends. And so most of all I stress to him, "Levi, you absolutely cannot say things like this. They are harmful. They are not true, and they do damage to people." We have a zero-tolerance policy for words and phrases like this.

In the end, I don't have the luxury of not being didactic. I don't have the luxury of not spewing out feminist rhetoric and rants using now seemingly overused terms such as "patriarchy" and "misogyny." And quite honestly, no one else should have that luxury either. Because the fact of the matter is that in 2016 and again in 2024, the United States citizenry elected a racist misogynist as president. Many let "locker room talk" be brushed off as an expected and harmless part of man-hood. And while Hollywood finally started serving justice to some of its own who had a long history of sexual harassment and assault offenses, white men in America started posting to social media about the witch-hunt in progress, lamenting that it was a dangerous time to be male—especially a white male. Our president-elect was, not surprisingly, at the helm of these complaints after making his statement that "It is a very scary time for young men in America" (Beckwith 2018).

I can say with confidence that it has been a very scary time to be a queer mom of a young boy in America, for I feel desperate in my need to have him grow up aware of his privilege and be willing to use it to create a more equitable world for women and minorities. The more our Supreme Court rolls back rights for women and LGBTQIA+ people, the scarier it gets. Despite the evidence on the government sanctioned document—the birth certificate—that we are both Levi's moms, we have been living in quiet fear that those rights and privileges might be taken from us, that someone might say our son belongs only to the one from whose womb he emerged.

Lately Levi has taken to describing himself as a "tough guy." This is only one phrase among many that he has inevitably picked up outside of our house—at school, from *Henry Danger*, or from one of the other silly and seemingly innocuous shows that are broadcast to our sons. He walks around hoisting his arms up in cactus shape, flexing his "muscles." He'll tilt his head toward one bicep and gently kiss it while grinning away. He giggles and seems to know that this is just child's play, that it isn't real, and most importantly that strength doesn't belong to him simply because he's a white man. He has experienced Ramona's strength and knows that Pippi can flex her muscles too, and so can his mommy and Didi.

As he drops his arms and dissolves into laughter, I imagine him laughing at gender, knowing that while the world has centered gender and masculinity in particular, our family doesn't. And I hope he continues to remind me of this for years to come.

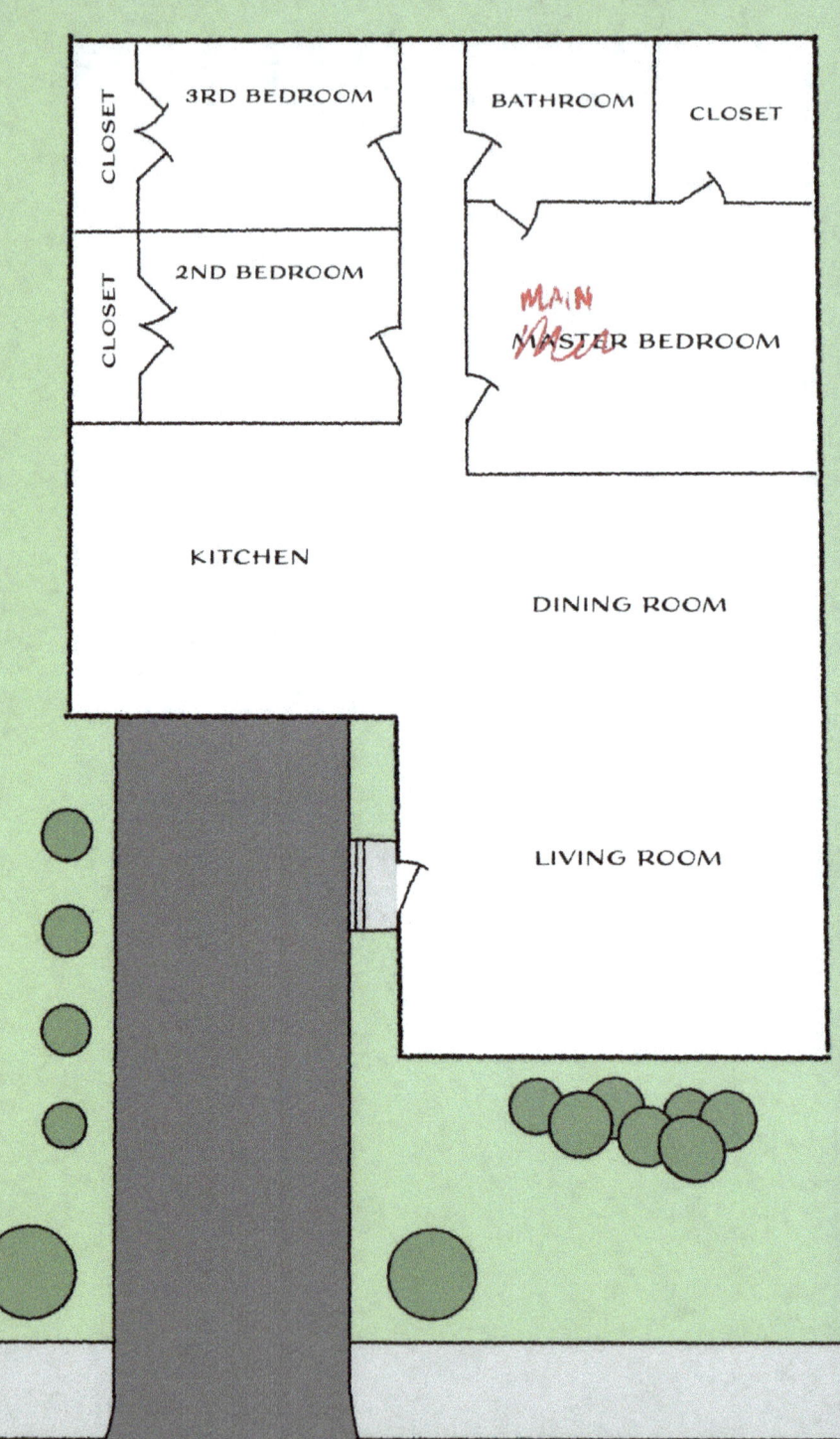

INTERVIEW: ANGIE RUNDLE
by Gail Marlene Schwartz

I met Angie through one of our open calls for submissions. She struck me immediately as a passionate, confidant, loving parent and booklover. Angie and I spoke over Zoom, which I recorded, and I edited the transcription with her approval. What follows are Angie's words.

♂

I AM A LIBRARIAN-LESBRARIAN at a public library in St. Louis County, Missouri. In my spare time, I sing in a queer women's chorus; the last theme was banned books. I also curate area Little Free Libraries. I have one son, Christopher, who is 22. I had him when I was a single teen mom. I was so young that he came to college with me! That experience shaped how liberal and accepting he is.

I was 26 when I came out, just out of college. It was hard on my mom; she couldn't understand because I had been in straight relationships that she saw as a success. I had been away at school, but she was seeing me as the person I was when I left. She didn't understand ... I had learned new things, developed new interests, exposed myself to more people. I had changed. Most of my friends in college were gay, and I have always been a theater kid, active in musicals, theater, and dance.

One day when Christopher was in first grade, we went out to breakfast. He said loud enough for the whole restaurant to hear, "There's a table with gay boys over there. Do you know them?" I quietly explained that, no, your mom doesn't know every gay person in this town. But in his brain, I did. Isn't that how a community works? Don't we just walk around campus [being] friends with every queer person?

I wanted to make sure he had positive male role models. My dad died when Christopher was three, and he doesn't have any meaningful memories of him. The first Father's Day after my dad was gone, Christopher's preschool teacher asked me how I would like to handle it. She suggested he make a gift for me, but what we ultimately decided was much better: My brothers are much younger than me and closer in age to Christopher, so he would make two gifts for "Uncle's Day" instead of Father's Day. We've been celebrating "Uncles Day" on the third Sunday in June ever since. Someone told him once, "You have to get two

Mother's Day gifts? That sucks," and he replied, "But I never have to get anything for Father's Day!"

Christopher was an Eagle Scout, and he was always active … We had an amazing experience with them. My ex-wife was a leader in Scouts, and they welcomed us with open arms. At summer camp, everyone knew that Christopher had two moms, and it was no big deal. Dads made themselves available to him, his friends' dads. Though he's 22 now, he still goes snowboarding with [one of those] friend[s] and the friend's dad. They kind of took him in, like, "Let's do some guy stuff." They play in the woods and make up games and sports, activities that aren't my thing.

I got married when Christopher was 10. [My former partner and I] are divorced now … but for 12 years he has had two moms. If you ask him about his parents, he will say he has a mom and a stepmom. She's still a very big part of his life—holidays, vacations, [and] birthdays, [and] we are friendly. Now I've been re-partnered for six years.

[My son] told me once that in a high school civics class he got paired with another kid who was doing the NRA as a topic. That kid wore a shirt that said "LGBT: Liberty, Guns, Beer, Trump." Christopher told me how he ended up with this kid [and said], "I didn't say anything—I just couldn't relate to him." He meant, "I don't know how to engage with toxic masculinity."

My son had feminist parenting. When asked about it, he said, "I never knew my mom was a feminist. I just knew your values … I knew you had never said 'I don't know how to do this'; you'd just figure it out."

He learned that moms just figure it out, [yet] he never considered it until he got older. Then he would hear things from his classmates or other places and think, *Oh, maybe my mom is different [from] other moms.* That was the point when he realized a lot of his experiences were really different.

My background in education shaped my parenting. I never talked down to Christopher, [and] I'd slip tidbits in during a teachable moment. For example, [when] we were looking at a house [with the sign], "Master bedroom," I'd say "Main bedroom" instead. I'm always learning and always teaching. I've always had him be responsible, even for "female" chores. He was responsible for cutting the grass and also for helping with laundry. One rule is that everyone helps out in the kitchen. Now he's living with his girlfriend, and he does 100 percent of the cooking. He doesn't see it as "less than" or as women's work, most likely because he's seen women do all the jobs imaginable in a household.

[He once shared with me] a memory he had. We were in the car—myself, my wife, Christopher, and his two girl cousins who were a few years younger than him. He was maybe 10 or 11, and they were seven and nine. On the drive, the girls asked him who his favorite mom to do different things with was, like to cook dinner with, to go to the movies with, to dance with. To that he responded, "What kind of dancing?" One mom likes fast dancing, the other mom likes choreographed dancing. These were genuine questions. They wanted to know more about his life with two moms. [He told them] I am the touchy-feely mom, and his other mom is the soccer mom, the sporty Boy Scout leader. He can connect with her that way. They [go] rock climbing and [have] their own special activities, things [I'm not] interested in. He didn't hesitate in answering any of their questions.

Christopher exclusively wore sweatpants and gym shorts for years. Such a boy! He's smart, so he would shower the night before and put on whatever clean clothes he was wearing to school the next day. This started early, like in kindergarten; he wanted to wear gym shorts. So I made a deal with him: "If you wear what I put out Monday through Thursday, you can wear what you want on Friday." This was until fourth or fifth grade when I got sick of fighting him. As long as he was clean, I let him wear what he wanted. He just wouldn't want to get rid of dirty things, even if they were smelly! He never had any questions about his gender, but he always knew I was open.

We read tons of books; we were always reading. The main characters were sometimes queer. *Better Nate Than Ever* is one. The main character is in middle school, and he goes to New York to audition and sees two boys kissing. I always asked questions while we read to make sure he understood. It was a great place for conversation. I might ask him, "Do you ever think about that?" It opened things up for a lot of discussion.

I remember one time when he was in eighth grade, one of my friends put this anecdote on Facebook for International Women's Day: A boy [is] in a car with his dad, and they [get] into an accident. The dad die[s], but the boy goes to the hospital. In surgery, the doctor says, "I can't operate on this boy because he's my son." When I told Christopher, he said, "Oh, that's easy: He has two dads!"

I said, "No, that's not it."

Then he said, "One is a dad, one is the stepdad, but he calls them both Dad."

"Nope."

Then he overthought. Was it a cloning thing? Did the dad fake his own death?

Finally, I said it's because the surgeon is his mother.

"Oh! I couldn't think of that. So easy! Why didn't I think of that?"

My child with two capable mothers couldn't figure out that the doctor was a mother. When I told him about this recently, he laughed so hard.

Many of his friends are gay or gender nonconforming. His girlfriend has lots of theater friends. He never asks stupid questions; he knows how to be kind. It's almost like street cred with his friends that his mom is gay. It sends a message like, "You're safe with me."

Christopher has said to me, "I know I have the privilege of being a straight white man." He tries to use it for other people.

I [once] asked him, "What would you do if police were harassing a person of color?"

He said he would step in, but if someone said, "That's so gay," he would get up and move. He thinks it's just not worth trying to argue.

His girlfriend said it's actually a running joke with their friends that he's the way he is because he has two moms. One big thing about him is that he never makes negative comments about menstruation; it's just a thing that bodies do. He also doesn't use the word "bitch" to refer to a female, even when he's in a group where it's being used. The other guys they're friends with say it without thinking, but he loves women and wouldn't want them to be called that. He's also pro-fat and pro-whatever the hell size you are. Occasionally, his girlfriend will say she shouldn't eat something or shouldn't eat too much of a "bad" food, and he reminds her that food is good and she can eat whatever she wants without judgment.

Christopher's friends and classmates trust him not to be a bigot or a homophobe. When he was in his first year at Mizzou and in the dorms, his friend Lu was being harassed for being gay and nonbinary, so Christopher let Lu stay in his room for the night so they felt safe. This is just one example of how who he is makes me so proud, not just as a mother but as a queer mother of a son.

GUY TIME

by Gail Marlene Schwartz

"I'm proud of you, Brother," says Erin, pulling my tween into a rough hug.

I hear Alexi's child voice, muffled by Erin's shoulder: "I loved our visit, especially cutting down the tree."

Behind them is said tree, in Erin's condo and adorned with blinking red lights and ornaments, some from our collection, some from Erin's. I'm grinning at the sight of their embrace. At nearly 12, my son is just inches shorter than my "boyfriend," a word we use because it sounds teenage-y and full of hormones, not because Erin, who identifies as nonbinary, feels so much like a boy.

Erin's and my relationship is just seven months old, but he is the only person I've felt serious about since Lucie and I broke up years ago, the only person

167

I've introduced to Alexi.

Coincidentally, Alexi's therapist told Lucie and me recently that she felt our boy needed a male role model. "That's straight people for you," said a lesbian friend, shaking her head. But despite my queer feminism, what the therapist said resonated.

Alexi is struggling with fears of growing up; he's resistant to talking about puberty, the future, or anything related. His counselor suggested he's afraid to be an adult because he has no idea what growing up looks like for him—other than separation from us—because before Erin, there were no men in our inner circle.

So how do I, a queer mom of a son, take care of his need, especially as a feminist woman who feels responsible for progressive social change? I had in fact thought of this before Lucie and I decided to have kids. Although I had researched "sons of lesbian moms" prior to getting pregnant, and although that research indicated those boys were perfectly fine, when my ultrasound revealed a tiny penis, I wondered whether two moms could meet this child's needs.

In his early childhood, we dressed him in gender-neutral clothing; read him "girl," "boy," and "other" stories; and made sure he knew how to cook and clean. Of course two women are enough for a boy child, we reasoned. We thought we could transcend sex and gender by being committed feminists in our parenting. But I also knew from anti-racism work how important it is for kids to see happy, well-adjusted, and successful people who look like them. And it was undeniable that

Alexi's body did not look like ours.

Perhaps my subconscious had this information in mind when I fell in love with Erin. It made sense, given my bisexuality and feminism, that although I picked someone to love who the world sees as a man, I also picked someone with a real mix of femininity and masculinity, someone who doesn't, in fact, identify as a man. *Is it possible*, I wondered, *that integrating Erin could give Alexi something—the role model that feels so important right now—but also take something else away—the feminist values we've been trying so hard to instill?*

♂

ON THE FIRST DAY OF Erin's visit, Alexi is like a man magnet. Within the first hour, my boy starts indicating that he's "with" Erin.

We show our guest the pool, and my kid is off and running. "Come on Erin, let's go swimming!" "Erin's on my team!" "I want to play pool volleyball, boys against girls." For a kid with nontraditional gender conditioning at home, he seems hyperaware of the physical similarities between them.

On the second day of Erin's visit, Alexi tells us, "Erin and I are going for a drive for some guy time. Don't expect us back soon." I check Erin's face to see whether this plan had been completely conceived and hatched by my boy, but Erin looks strangely pleased.

Later we watch *Jurassic Park*, and Alexi holds Erin's hand while they're both sitting on the couch. In the pool, they have a splashing fight, and then Alexi climbs on Erin's back. Watching the two together reminds me of a comedy team, Laurel and Hardy or Fry and Laurie.

When we decide to play charades, Alexi immediately grabs Erin's hand and says, "Boys against girls!" I start wondering whether Alexi's hunger for a male role model is about our failure to truly embody feminist values and gender liberation.

♂

I HAVE A HEART-TO-HEART with Erin after the Christmas visit. Had Lucie and I failed? Was Alexi's glomming onto him evidence that queer moms simply cannot give a boy what he needs?

"Well, the way I see it," he says, "there are three things going on."

I sit back in my armchair and reach out for his hand.

"There's sex, there's gender, and there's sexual orientation. With sex, he sees the difference between you and Lucie and him. Alexi sees me as the same as him in this very fundamental physical way. He has to figure out what that means."

His palm is warm against mine, and I'm listening.

"With gender, he sees someone who loves therapy and can be emotionally vulnerable, because that's who I am. He sees someone who learns on his own with YouTube videos, whether it's woodworking or sewing, canning or computers. Because that's who I am. He sees a whole mix of qualities, and hopefully that will translate into him knowing he can express all of who *he* is."

Yes.

"And with sexual orientation, well, that's pretty simple. He knows people who are attracted to the same gender, to a different gender, and to many genders. He's seeing that there's no one right way to be. You can't tell someone that and have them get it. But he's not being told; he's around it. I think that's the best way to learn."

♂

ON OUR ZOOM CHECK-IN, Alexi says how excited he is about spending Christmas Eve at the hotel all together. I'm envisioning us playing "Ode to Joy" on the mandolin and piano, unwrapping the matching PJs I bought, munching on cocktail shrimp, and playing Throw Throw Burrito with sparkly Christmas music in the background. But most of all, I'm imagining watching Alexi looking at Erin the way he used to look at me.

Perhaps seeing us, a tall broad-shouldered woman and a smaller gender-ambiguous person with a penis, can mean for Alexi a more complicated relationship with gender, a more open and easy connection with all of himself. Maybe having Erin in his life means he will emerge with a healthy sense of his own identity as a man, or as whatever gender he ends up identifying with, with a deep respect and appreciation for people of all genders. Maybe it doesn't have to mean a shortcoming in his queer moms or how they brought him into the world.

Or maybe it just means he has a teammate when we play charades. And frankly, that's more than enough for me to feel massively grateful.

A PUNK PLAYLIST FOR QUEER MOMS RAISING FEMINIST BOYS
By Jolivette Mecenas

At the height of anti-Asian violence during the pandemic, a small joy took over the internet: The Linda Lindas, a punk band of teen and tween girls from my Los Angeles neighborhood, went viral with their song "Racist, Sexist Boy." Performing at the local library for AAPI heritage month, the girls rocked the stacks and the small crowd of masked-up librarians. Guitarists Bella Salazar and Lucia de la Garza pounded out buzzsaw chords while bassist Eloise Wong and her cousin, 10-year-old drummer Mila de la Garza, growled their intersectional callout of playground misogyny.

Everyone in our family—myself, my partner Charlyne, and our nine-year-old son, whom I'll henceforth refer to as "the kid"—were already big fans. Our son's first concert was an all-ages punk show organized by

Eloise's parents to fundraise for the music program at her Chinatown public school, with local folk/punk legends Phranc, Alice Bag, and Mike Watt. Charlyne fangirls to "Claudia Kishi," the Linda Linda's poppy tribute to everyone's favorite Japanese American character in *The Babysitters Club* books, which she read as a kid. And I thought the girls' performance of Bikini Kill's "Rebel Girl" was the best part of the girl-power movie *Moxie* on Netflix. Anti-racist, anti-sexist, intergenerational music-and-troublemaking, and community-based activism for public education—the Linda Lindas model values that Charlyne and I teach our child to help him be present with a full heart. Our intention is especially important for our cis-gendered son who moves through the world with the raucous physicality and energy of, well, a stereotypical "boy." In sisterhood, I offer this punk playlist for queer moms doing their best to raise feminist boys.

Track #1: "Racist, Sexist Boy" by The Linda Lindas

THE KID AND I RECENTLY rocked out to the viral video again. "Do you remember what this song is about?" I asked him.

"Yeah, a boy she knew told her that his dad told him to stay away from people from China. That's racist."

"Yup. And what about the word 'sexist'?"

"That's when you have stereotypes against girls. And say mean things about them."

The kid gave two thumbs up and an approving smile.

Track #2: "Violet" by Hole

APPROXIMATELY A YEAR INTO virtual school for our family, and a few months before The Linda Lindas took over the world, the bottom fell out of our delusion that the kid was doing just fine learning fourth grade entirely online. "He seems distracted, like he's looking at something else during class," his teacher reported in our parent conference. He was also having a lot more meltdowns during Zoom school. During one such emotional collapse, I tried to help the kid by searching his laptop web browser for a missing homework assignment. I found it—along with a link to a website with the completely unimaginative title "PRINCESS PEACH RIDES BIG DICK."

I clicked on it, and sure enough, there was an animated, pink-frocked Princess Peach from the Nintendo Super Mario world being "rescued" by the mustachioed Mario. I clicked on another link on the browser history, which led me to live-action adults in costume as Mario and Princess Peach. Cosplay porn is a *thing*. Another link led to Sonic the Hedgehog with a "female" hedgehog; clearly, every link was the result of the kid searching for the cartoonish video game characters he was obsessed with. But the internet is gonna internet, and the algorithm led him to animated hedgehog erotica, with real people and real sex acts in the banner ads. Clicking on every suspect link spanning the previous two weeks, my heart sank with every blowjob and every wide-eyed woman (real or animated) eager to comply. To be clear, we thought we had set controls to block adult content from browser searches, but obviously we bombed on this essential parenting skill. With this pervasive shitty content, how do boys learn not to just take what they want? And how do girls learn how to say no?

Track #3: "Suggestion" by Fugazi

AS TWO MOMS OF A BOY, what is our interpretation of what it means to be a man?

Back in 1988, Fugazi's "Suggestion" forced men in the testosterone-amped punk scene to think about their interpretation of manhood, and how being complicit observers of sexual harassment and assault factored into that identity. As hailed in *Pitchfork*, lead singer Ian MacKaye raged about the "aggressive objectification of women's bodies," singing from the perspective of a woman (Anderson 2016). In her book *Boys & Sex*, journalist Peggy Orenstein writes that "... the media scripts boys consume from childhood onward are continuously objectifying, demeaning, hostile, inimical, or indifferent to women and present masculinity as inherently antagonistic to femininity" (Orenstein 2020). We are working hard to flip these scripts through co-ed sports and activities that foster cooperation and competition with girls, and with other boys and nonbinary kids, including swimming, karate, baseball, and hip-hop dance.

But Orenstein points out the persistent influence of the media on boys' understanding of gender, and during our COVID year of childless contact, the kid—like all of us—consumed a lot of media. I remember listening to an interview with Orenstein when her book came out in early 2020 while on the elliptical at the gym right before shutdown. I made a mental note to get a copy, so I'd be ready when we needed to have the porn talk (inevitable and necessary, according to Orenstein) with our son *years* down the road, when he was, like, 12. The kid's increased internet time brought on by COVID hastened this plan, and now I was panic-searching the internet for advice.

Track #4: "Johnny Hit and Run Pauline" by X and Track #5: "Keep on Livin'" by Le Tigre

CHARLYNE WAS DEVASTATED when I showed her what I found. She, too, went through every link. How were we going to talk to him without freaking out and shaming him? When it comes to family culture, Charlyne and I have a lot in common. Both of us have parents who immigrated from the Philippines, settling in L.A. in the 1970s – 1980s. Busy working and figuring out life in their new country, our parents did not explain 1980s media, like *Porky's* and *Fast Times at Ridgemont High*. The only "sex talk" was a singular message hammered into all Catholic girls: Don't have sex until marriage, and (as a concession to reality) don't get pregnant. I got the latter message on repeat from puberty onward, as my parents worried that I would screw up my chances at college and a future by making them young grandparents. The irony was not lost on me when I started dating, with zero chance of being impregnated by my high school and college girlfriends (though I did also date men). As we reflected on the messages we remembered from our childhood, Charlyne pointed out the main theme: "Nothing was ever sex positive."

We sat down with our son with a mission: *no shaming*.

"Do you know what sex is?" I began.

"Umm, yes …" he mumbled, fidgeting. "Sex is not gender?" Inwardly I fist-pumped, *Yes!* Our chats on gender à la Judith Butler had sunk in (Butler 2006).

"Yes, that's true, but I'm talking about when two people *have* sex. That's different. A man and a woman can agree to have sex. Two men can have sex. Two women can have sex …"

"Like you and Mom?"

I looked at Charlyne. Her eyes widened. Images from the porn sites flashed in the space between us. "Uh, yes. Like me and Mom. But that's different. We love each other. *Those* are actors." I was making things up as I went here. I took a deep breath. "You saw a lot of images and videos that are hard to understand, because they're for grownups. When grownups agree to have sex, they agree what that looks like. But for kids, it's hard to understand these videos, and it might even be scary."

"It's not your fault you found them, though. We're sorry you watched them," Charlyne jumped in. There were more questions, hugs, agreements, and more hugs. We were doing the hard work of flipping those scripts into an age-appropriate understanding of sex positive.

Interlude: Talking about sex positively and responsibly with my young son is life or death for me. I did date a few boys and men when I was younger, all good guys. I was also assaulted in the mosh pit of a punk show when I was 22. I was with a buddy of mine, Rick. We had just graduated from college and were stoked to finally see the band X play in an intimate Hollywood club. Rick, a soon-to-be high school art teacher also from L.A., had sandy blond hair and a body toned from surfing. I remember watching him hurling around in the pit like a gleeful maniac, while I was smashed against other bodies, my arms pinned to the sides of my petite 5'2" frame. I couldn't move. And that's when some fucker started penetrating me from behind. Sure, it could've been a woman, but I doubt it. There weren't many women in the pit. My faceless assailant pushed his hand into me with a force that made me stop breathing for a minute. And I still couldn't move my arms or even turn my head. I just had to take it. When the song ended, the pit loosened up, and I stumbled out, numb. Later, when Rick and I found each other after the show, I didn't tell him. I didn't tell anyone for about twenty years, the memory a grave excavated in therapy. I sing Le Tigre's song "Keep on Livin'" when that shitty memory and stories of girls and women being assaulted and harassed bring me back to that mosh pit. Consent is sex positive, and so is teaching your son not to rape.

Track #6: "Racist, Sexist Boy" (redux) by The Linda Lindas

HONESTLY, I CAN'T remember exactly what we said to communicate to our son that women are often seen as objects in porn, and that's not okay. Charlyne remembers that the week we had the porn talk with him, six Asian women were shot dead at the suburban Atlanta spas where they worked by a 21-year-old white man who killed them to excise his sex addiction (Hagen 2021). That man believed some fucked up misogynistic and racist messaging that is the norm in our culture that stripped away the humanity of those six women. As a result, the murderer believed it was his right to execute six working class Asian women so he could rid himself of his objects of temptation. The messages that shaped the murderer are the same messages bombarding our young boy. As his parents, we fight back with our own role models. Recue the Linda Lindas calling out all the racist, sexist boys and men as meanie, fake jerks.[1]

Track #7: "Want" by Jawbreaker

IN *BOYS & SEX*, AND ITS predecessor *Girls & Sex*, (Orenstein 2017) Orenstein interviews dozens of boys and girls who believe that porn is instructional. *How awful, I thought, to be a young person today and model your intimacy and vulnerability with another person on Pornhub, where dead-eyed actors fucked along a spectrum of mechanical boredom on one end and, in the language of the boys interviewed by Orenstein, "rapey" on the other end.* Hell no, do I wish that sexuality for my son. I want him to know that yes, what he sees in porn are acts that consenting partners can choose to do, but those acts are not a one-size-fits-all model for sex and intimacy.

---

[1] The actual lyrics are charming in their innocence, but copyright laws prohibit me from quoting them without permission in this essay, so go listen to the song yourself!

Mutual respect and communication between partners are the (hot) foundations of sexual education. When Blake Schwarzenbach, the lead singer of Jawbreaker, growls out his desire to his interlocutor in "Want," he is being sweetly sincere, pioneering the emo genre of pop-punk.

But this message about hot consent is for a future sex talk, part two, when the kid is older. For now, I'm happy to report that our son finished 4th grade. His current media consumption: books by his favorite chapter book author Stuart Gibbs and Netflix cartoons about a speedy racing snail and about a dinosaur amusement park gone awry. He likes to search online for Pokémon cards and new recipes to bake (up next: banana cream pie).

Most importantly, we finally figured out how to properly set parental controls on the computer. And, after COVID restrictions lifted, and the kid went back to school in person, our little family sang along with Bella, Lucia, Eloise, and Mila—now all in their teens—at an all-ages Linda Lindas show. Punk's not dead—it just got better with girls in the front.

ABOUT THE CONTRIBUTORS

ADA MALONE TEACHES ESL at a high school in New York. Her academic work has been published in both the *Journal of Interactive Technology and Pedagogy* and *Forum*. She coproduced the documentary film *Con Job: Stories of Adjunct and Contingent Labor*, published by Computers and Composition Digital Press and winner of the Michelle Kendrick Outstanding Digital Production/ Scholarship Award. Her ebook *Are We There Yet? Computers and the Teaching of Writing in American Higher Education—20 Years Later*, coauthored with James P. Purdy, was published in 2021 by Computers and Composition Digital Press. Ada has recently returned to her first writing love, creative nonfiction, and is working on a collection of micro-memoirs about motherhood. She and her wife have a ten-year-old son whom they are raising to be a loving feminist.

Ada's Feminist Journey

I WAS RAISED BY AN ANTI-FEMINIST. My stay-at-home mother felt as if her life choices were under attack by feminists. She would scoff at the mention of Betty Friedan, and smoke would come out of her ears should someone bring up Gloria Steinem. Our house never saw an issue of *Ms.* magazine; instead, *Family Circle, Good Housekeeping,* and *Reader's Digest* arrived with our mail. I was taught that feminists were coming to destroy the family. They were saying women could have it all, and my mother maintained we simply could not (perhaps she was right about that part). I followed in her footsteps and turned my nose up at feminism. Who needed feminism in the '80s and '90s anyway? I wore whatever I wanted, and in school I felt I was treated equally to my male class-mates. Women voted and Geraldine Ferraro ran for office. Feminism was dead and unnecessary in my mind.

I saw feminism as a dirty F-word until late in my college years. I didn't see myself as a feminist, though I wanted to be seen as a "tough girl." In college, this tough girl image eventually grew into fashioning myself as a tomboy because I could clearly see it was better to be a "boy" in the world, but I couldn't think of a way to actually name or confront that notion other than in a kind of "if you can't beat 'em, join 'em" way. I shaved my head, continued to wear my combat boots, and bought an army jacket from the Army Navy store to go with them. I bought even baggier clothes to obscure my breasts and, quite nicely by default I thought, my little pot belly, and I prided myself on the fact that I didn't have a waist and hips like a woman—instead my body went straight down on the sides like a boy's body. I beamed when retail workers would accidentally mistake me for a man and then trip over their apologies (*Please*, I would think in my head, *this is all by design*).

I have no doubt that some of this gender expression exploration was also related to the fact that I had yet to come out of the closet, but mostly it was due to the implied knowledge that making my way in the world would be easier the more masculine I could be. But the fact is that I am not masculine and have no desire to be. I'm more femme on the gender spectrum, and trying to perform a gender that wasn't my own became exhausting and uncomfortable. Eventually, I began to see the folly in my thinking. How unfair was it that I had to reshape myself to be more masculine in order to make my way in the world? Why should it be better to be male? The problem was with the system, I came to realize, not with my gender.

And so, I became a feminist. I kept my head shaved but wore dresses with no bra and (often) no shoes. I stopped shaving because that was patriarchal BS. But most of all, I studied. I went back to my critical theory textbooks and studied feminism. When I went to graduate school, I helped bring Gloria Steinem to campus. I read *Ms.* and *Bust* magazines. Suddenly, the world came into focus, and not in an entirely good way. I began to see clearly how far we still had to go to achieve equality, respect, and consent as women. I began to understand there was more to gender equality than being out of the house and wearing pants.

Recently, I pulled up behind a hotrod at a stop light. The back window contained a huge decal that read, "Yeah, it makes the panties drop" with an image of a woman's legs spread with a pair of tiny underwear around the ankles. Around the license plate was a holder that read, "Drop the mother fuckin' pantys [*sic*]." This car had managed to get in front of me by passing me on the right in a roar of acceleration (only, of course, to be in the same spot as me at the next red light). Lest we think feminism is no longer necessary, as I did in my youth, lest we believe we've done enough or cannot do better, we need only look as far as the car in front of us or at the president of the United States. In looking at my own son, I want to do better. I pledge to do differently.

Gail Marlene Schwartz is a writer and freelance editor for a variety of clients, including Aplomb Consulting, Publish Your Purpose, and Nectar Communications. She is the author of the novel *Falling Through the Night* (Demeter Press), winner of the National Indie Excellence Award in 2024 in the LGBTQIA+ fiction category. Gail's other books include *My Sister's Girlfriend, The Loudest Bark,* and *Clementine in Quarantine*. She is a founding editor of the online journal, *Hotch Potch Literature and Art*, and has been published in numerous literary magazines and anthologies. Gail is the proud queer mom of a teenage boy, whom she is raising with both her partner, who identifies as nonbinary, and her best friend, her son's other mom.

Gail's Feminist Journey

WHEN I WAS GROWING UP, my mother was president of the local chapter of the National Council of Jewish Women. She also had a personality disorder. These two facts were both critical in my development as a feminist and a leader.

My mother was capable in many ways and took on leadership in Jewish feminist circles, modeling a way to be a leader and a feminist. In spite of her life being very traditional as a middle-class Jewish housewife, she had this other world she inhabited that I was drawn to. I saw that even though my mother had less power than my father, she was able to join with other women and use her skills to uplift everyone. I wanted to do that too.

I also suffered profound trauma from growing up

with a mentally ill parent. Because of her illness, my mother wasn't able to nurture my sister and me. She looked to me for comfort and caretaking, and because I wasn't able to provide it, she lashed out in cruel and damaging ways. It's taken me years to get to the point where I've been able to have healthy relationships of my own, and I still deal with panic, anxiety, and other relics of childhood. In my healing, I've confronted psychiatric labels that are really just words we have for problems stemming from past suffering. Because women have suffered profoundly due to patriarchy, I have no doubt that patriarchy is mixed in with other causes of my mother's illness. In healing myself, I've looked at systems theory and oppression. Feminism, humanism, and intersectionality have all been part of understanding how to be well in a culture that values white over other races, male over other genders, straight over other orientations, and so on. Political action has always been part of what I'm doing in the world, part and parcel with personal transformation.

Having a son has offered me the chance to work on these issues from a completely different vantage point. My ex and I wanted Alexi to grow from a place of connection and love rather than harshness and alienation. We used attachment parenting to raise our child: We wore him in a sling, co-slept, and breastfed him for two years. He's never been punished; instead, we've had weekly family meetings when we problem-solve issues together. He has many choices about his life, and we respect his feelings and preferences whenever possible. This is a massive contrast with my own childhood, during which, from the day I came home from the hospital, I was in my own room in a crib while my parents utilized the "cry it out" approach. I wasn't allowed in my parents' bed, and I grew up drinking from a bottle. I was punished, belted, and sent away for eight weeks every summer to a camp where I was bullied mercilessly. My son is confident and happily goes to sleep when he's tired. He's affectionate, confident, and emotionally intelligent, and he connects with people easily. I am insecure and often sleep fitfully, and I struggle with isolation and take medication for OCD.

My feminism has certainly led to personal evolution, and I feel I've done my share to heal generational trauma. I hope my son continues the work. Telling my story and our stories through these essays and interviews is an important first step.

June BlueSpruce lives with her wife in Seattle, where they raised their two sons, now grown. Her essays have appeared in *Whiteness Is Not an Ancestor: Essays on Life and Lineage by White Women*; *Sacred Stone, Sacred Water: Women Writers and Artists Encounter Ireland*; *Catamaran Literary Reader*; and the chapbook *Coming Home; and HerStry*. Her poems have been published in *Sisters Singing: Blessings, Prayers, Art, Songs, Poetry, and Sacred Stories by Women*; *My Lover Is a Woman: Contemporary Lesbian Love Poems*; and journals including *off our backs*. June writes about healing, spirituality, and social change on her blog at: https://www.junebluespruce.com/blog/.

Irina González is an editor, journalist, and future social worker currently pursuing her MSW at the University of Denver. As a sober bisexual Latina mom with ADHD, she writes about parenting, mental health, social justice, and intersectional neurodivergent families. With 20 years of experience in women's media, her work has appeared in over 50 national publications. She's written 100+ essays featured in *The Washington Post*, *Latina* magazine, *Yahoo*, *HuffPost*, *Parents*, *Good Housekeeping*, *Oprah Daily*, *Real Simple*, *What to Expect*, *Glamour*, *Business Insider*, and more. She writes the Parenting in Hard Mode newsletter and created the limited-series Pandemic Mama podcast. She's a Cuban/Russian immigrant who grew up in Florida, spent most of her adult life in New York City, and now lives in Colorado with her partner, rambunctious kiddo, and their fur babies.

http://irinagonzalez.com/.

Amy Hinze-Pifer (she/her) lives in the Midwest US with her wife, two kids, and their very large dog.

Marie Holmes is the parenting reporter at HuffPost. Her work has appeared in *Scary Mommy*, *Cosmopolitan*, *The Washington Post,* and other publications. She was awarded an Emerging Writer Fellowship at the Center for Fiction. She lives with her family in New York City.

Marie's Feminist Journey

I am the daughter of a female OB/GYN who provided abortion care. I am a lesbian, and I am a mother. My feminism is rooted in my body—in my right to decide who, if, and when.

When the Supreme Court overturned *Roe v. Wade*, as we knew since November 8, 2016 they would do, I felt helpless. My votes hadn't mattered, my small campaign contributions hadn't mattered, and my marching in a pink pussy hat knit by my friend's mother hadn't mattered. I wanted to curl up in bed and chew on my cynicism and sorrow. I wanted to wallow. But I have kids. And so sometimes, even when I feel like all hope has been wrung out of me, I have to pretend for their sake, to sell them on the future like the narrator of that poem "Good Bones" by Maggie Smith that we all keep posting on social media because it rings so achingly true. I feel compelled to rationalize having brought them into this world.

So, I bribed them with pizza and made them put on their shoes. We picked up one of their friends on our way downtown and showed up in Washington Square Park.

No signs, no matching green clothing, just me and three children. My eight-year-old daughter doesn't quite understand what an abortion is, only that it means not being forced to have a baby. My son, who is almost 13, became pro-choice a few months back when I explained that abortion was the thing that would save a kid his age from having to become a parent. Then his best friend, Gabrielle, who had just turned 13 and had her period for only a matter of months, was, as usual, goofing around with my son. But she was also content to stand quietly and watch the crowd, reading the signs and listening to the chants. *They will remember being here on this day*, I thought, and it felt like a small triumph. My son Max has long blond hair and is constantly being misgendered, an occurrence that he meets with a shrug. Gabrielle is a mix of Black and white and wears her hair in a beautiful crown of curls. The crowd was very much theirs: racially mixed, ambiguously gendered, and so, so young.

When my mother started bringing me to abortion rights rallies, I was around ten years old. "Women united will never be defeated!" we chanted. The chant has changed, at least in the crowd that gathered under the arch that day. It's now, "The people united will never be defeated!" The vibe was very gender inclusive. "People will die" read one sign, and I thought, *That doesn't quite work*. It's not *all* people. It's a specific group of us, the same group that lives with the fear of being raped. We're not all women, but we are all oppressed, together.

We need a new word for us, for those of us bound together by the impact and injustice of this ruling. I don't know whether *misogyny* is the term for it, and I'm not sure that *feminism* is still the word for the way we fight back. I don't know whether a small, determined group of idealistic kids can prevent our democracy from crumbling, but I have faith that they will come up with new words. We've reclaimed *queer*, we've defined *cis*, and we've cracked open a space for *nonbinary*. My children's generation will find a new language. I may not know what to write on a sign, and I may show up empty-handed, but I will be there with them, present for our fight.

Speaker, author, film director/producer, and queer historian **Robin Lowey** seeks to elevate the discourse in our country about the role lesbian history plays in advancing LGBTQIA+ civil rights and social equity. Robin is the author of *Game Changers: Lesbians You Should Know About*. Now in its second printing, *Game Changers* won best LGBTQIA+ book in the Next Generation Indie Book Awards. As a pioneering queer parent and an activist, Robin's work focuses on LGBTQIA+ achievements that have advanced a more inclusive society, while seeking to address the unmet educational needs of a culture that continues to oppress queer people.

https://lesbiangamechangers.com/ourteam

Katherine Mack is a professor of English at the University of Colorado Springs. Her research is wide-ranging, encompassing truth and reconciliation efforts in South Africa, motherhood and family in the United States, the genre and practice of life writing, and rhetorical pedagogy in the era of "truth decay." Across these diverse sites, she aims to illuminate how the personal and life narratives function rhetorically, in ways that are both productive and problematic. Mack is the author of *From Apartheid to Democracy: The Truth and Reconciliation Commission of South Africa* (Penn State UP, 2014), *The Case for Single Motherhood: Contemporary Maternal Identities and Family Formations* (University of Alabama Press, 2024), as well as articles for academic journals and essays in edited collections. She is currently at work on a memoir, *A Life I Never Imagined,* about the power of heeding her internal compass and creating a marvelous, boisterous, and unconventional framily (her conscious merging of family and friends).

Lalita du Perron was born in Amsterdam and now lives in the San Francisco Bay Area. She has a PhD in South Asian Studies (SOAS, 2000) and is the Associate Director of the Center for South Asia at Stanford. She has published two books and a number of articles on the song texts of North Indian art music and is currently working on a project on consent. In a separate incarnation, Lalita performs and writes comedy as Lalita Dee (@lalitadeecomedy).

Devon Ward is a youth librarian living in the GTA, Ontario, Canada. She has two outrageous children that live with her part-time. She has no pets to list in an author bio, but rather a prolific spider plant, a moody but lovely garden every summer, and a bad book to bookshelf ratio, in the sense that there are too many books and not enough shelves.

Jolivette Mecenas hails from Los Angeles, where she spent her childhood and returned to after living abroad in San Francisco, New York, and Honolulu. She lives in the Eagle Rock neighborhood of L.A. with her partner Charlyne and their son. An English professor at California State University Dominguez Hills, she teaches courses in writing and rhetoric and directs the composition program. When she is not being very lazy, she is reading, playing music, hiking with her dogs, connecting with friends over dinner, and relaxing at the beach. She and the family love cheering on Shohei Ohtani and the Dodgers, playing board games, and travelling (up next: the Philippines).

<u>Jolivette's Feminist Journey</u>

These days I spend *hours* driving the carpool for three seventh grade boys—my kid and his two buddies. We drive from one end of Los Angeles to the other to get to their magnet school, traversing freeways during morning and afternoon commutes. It is an act of supreme parental dedication that requires strong coffee, snacks, and Zen-like meditation to be one with the Hollywood Freeway. I also get a peek into the world of 12-year-old boys.

Sometimes during their screen-sharing of video games, anime, or memes, one of them will protest, "Nah bro, that's sexist!" and the others will easily agree. I drive silently in wonder. Wow, we're raising feminist boys!

As a seventh grader in 1985, I was not a feminist, and I did not grasp sexism enough to be able to point it out to a fellow 12-year-old. I did, however, have a pretty solid understanding of what felt unfair. For instance, through-out childhood, I loved baseball. I practiced for hours by myself every weekend, ricocheting the ball against a wall to practice fielding grounders and "pitching" to myself to practice batting. But the local park league did not organize co-ed baseball teams. This felt tragically unfair. Lots of boys—my little brother even—dreamt of playing for the Dodgers, but for me to share that dream would be like announcing I wished to grow equine legs and race in the Kentucky Derby—too crazy. Sure, my parents would've signed me up for softball if I had asked, but no, that giant ball was weird. Besides, I loved baseball.

During a lunchtime baseball game in fifth grade, I, one of only two girls playing, came up to bat. The opposite team jeered. "A girl?" they asked. "Easy out!" Of course the batter gets razzed, that's baseball. But I felt extra contempt hurled at me while standing at home plate. All the outfielders moved in closer. No way a girl could hit hard. I squinted at the pitcher and choked up on the bat. The *thwack!* as I hit a solid line drive between second and third, good for a double and an RBI, still resounds in my ears 40 years later. As I rounded first, full speed to second base, the boys on my team cheered in giddy surprise. The second baseman was silent with respect as I beat the throw.

I love this first girl-power memory of saying, "In your face!" after being easily written off by others. But it did not magically transform me into a feminist, and I gave up baseball soon after.

By seventh grade, I started getting jeered at in a different way. After school, I'd wait for the city bus to take me home. Without fail, some truckful of grown men would slow down and make kissing noises at me or shout words that made me feel dirty and scared. What I understood at the time was that it was my fault for being a 12-year-old girl wearing a tank top and shorts on a hot day and sitting alone on a bus stop bench. I felt like I deserved to feel ashamed. I didn't tell my parents or anyone.

By the time I turned thirteen, some family members were always telling me not to get pregnant; that felt bad too. Shame was clearly connected to sex, but I started to feel ashamed for just existing in my body. Accidentally leak my period on my gym sweats at school? Mortifying! Even bra straps peeking out of my tank top was shameful, which meant it was shameful to have breasts, which was super confusing because it seemed like everyone loved boobs. If I sat with my legs relaxed at a family party, an uncle would point and say "Bukaka!" which, loosely translated from Tagalog, means "Your legs are spread apart, and you are sitting like a whore!" This used to be a common way to reprimand a young girl unwittingly sitting like she was asking to get fucked, and I would instantly cross my legs in shame. Fortunately, most Filipinos don't say this anymore because it's widely recognized as shitty;

feminist Filipinas have even reclaimed the *bukaka* stance.

After seventh grade, I did not have a positive relationship with my body. I disowned it mentally, which led to some terrible experiences as a young person, right up to my early twenties. The boundaries between yes/no, pleasure/shame, desire/fear, and consent/violation were fuzzy. Men—and some women—took advantage of what I told myself was a sex-positive attitude. By then I felt really bad. Depressed.

My girlfriend at the time passed along her copy of *Bastard Out of Carolina* by Dorothy Allison, a hard book to get through. But Allison gives language to difficult feelings. Up to that point, most of my reading focused on (mostly white) men doing or thinking "big" things in the world. I started to read differently. Besides Allison, I've learned much from other writers who have had difficult and also deeply and defiantly joyous experiences, including Audre Lorde, Jeannette Winterson, Maxine Hong Kingston, Gloria Anzaldúa, Toni Morrison, Virginia Woolf, Leslie Feinberg, Kate Bornstein, Alison Bechdel, Lynda Barry, bell hooks, Angela Davis, Cathy Park Hong, Zadie Smith, Deborah A. Miranda, Maggie Nelson, Rebecca Solnit, Michelle Tea, Sara Ahmad, Chanel Miller, and Alice Wong.

I became a feminist as a reader, student, and teacher; as a daughter, sister, aunt, mother, and partner; and as a young girl, a young woman, and now in my middle age. I became a feminist to survive. There are more stories to read, listen to, and learn from, more stories to write. I am still becoming a feminist, and I am still here.

ACKNOWLEDGEMENTS

Boyhood Reimagined was conceived initially out of conversations between us, Ada Malone and Gail Marlene Schwartz, two queer moms of sons. Our longstanding friendship, beginning at the farmhouse on Farnsworth Road in Colchester, Vermont, when we came out to one another, started a conversation that we continue each time we meet. So grateful for our relationship, both personal and working and everything in between.

Obviously, the book would not exist without our sons, Levi and Alexi. Boys, we adore you, we believe in you, we are inspired by you, and yes, even when we're frustrated by you. You have, in part, made us who we are. Thank you.

To our contributors and interviewees, Sam, June, Jolivette, Katherine, Emanuelle, Rosanne, Irina, Robin, Sabrina, Devon, Brooke, Amy, Marie, Elliot, Kate, Brie, Meadow, Jenn, Lalita, and Angie, wow, we could not have asked for more fabulous colleagues and collaborators. For those of you who attended monthly meetings, helped recruit participants, interviewed friends, and are helping get the word out about the project, well, just know that it simply wouldn't have happened without you. And, it certainly would not have been nearly as rich or vast in scope.

To our families, Dawn, Erin, and Lucie, we are eternally thankful for all of your support. Having you to talk with throughout the years of work helped us do and be our best.

And to Erin, who so generously and enthusiastically took on the visual art supporting this project, a very particular and enormous thank you. Your paintings, including the book cover, do more than jazz the book up—they take it out of the realm of academia and transform it into a work of art. We are so grateful.

To our publisher, Diane J. Windsor at Motina Books, we hit the jackpot with you! From day one, you've been clear, professional, supportive, nurturing, and the best partner we could ask for. Thank you for being a staunch ally and for believing in this book, in us, and in the collaborative process.

BIBLIOGRAPHY

Anderson, Stacey. "The Story of Feminist Punk in 33 Songs." *Pitchfork.com,* 8 August 2016.

Beckwith, Ryan Teague. "'A Scary Time for Young Men.' President Trump Decries Sexual Assault Allegations." Time. Oct. 2, 2018. https://time.com/5412955/donald-trump-says-scary-time-men-sexual-assault-allegations/.

Butler, Judith. *Gender Trouble: Feminism and the Subversion of Identity.* Routledge, 2006.

Daniels, Arlene Kaplan. 1987. "Invisible Work." *Social Problems* 34 (5): 403–415. https://doi.org/10.2307/800538.

Day, Shelbi. 2017. "LGBTQ Family Fact Sheet." Family Equality Council. https://www2.census.gov/cac/nac/meetings/2017-11/LGBTQ-families-factsheet.pdf.

Diamond, Jeremy. 2018. "Trump Says It's 'a Very Scary Time for Young Men in America.'" *CNN.com*. https://www.cnn.com/2018/10/02/politics/trump-scary-time-for-young-men-metoo/index.html.

Doyle, Glennon. 2022. *We Can Do Hard Things*. Season 1, episode 84, "Mothers & Sons with Ocean Vuong (and Chase Melton). On the Day Productions, April 24. Podcast, 64 min. https://momastery.com/blog/we-can-do-hard-things-ep-84/.

Drexler, Peggy, and Linden Gross. 2006. *Raising Boys Without Men: How Maverick Moms are Creating the Next Generation of Exceptional Men*. Rodale Books.

Ford, Clementine. 2019. *Boys Will Be Boys: Power, Patriarchy and Toxic Masculinity*. Oneworld Publications.

Gartrell, Nanette, and Henny Bos. 2010. "US National Longitudinal Lesbian Family Study: Psychological Adjustment of 17-Year-Old Adolescents." *Pediatrics* 126 (1): 28–36. https://doi.org/10.1542/peds.2009-3153.

Golombok, Susan. 2020. *We Are Family: The Modern Transformation of Parents and Children*. PublicAffairs.

Grossheinrich, Nicola, Julia Schaeffer, Christine Firk, Thomas Eggermann, Lynn Huestegge, and Kerstin Konrad. 2022. "Childhood Adversity and Approach/Avoidance-Related Behaviour in Boys." *Journal of Neural Transmission* 129 (4): 421-429. https://doi.org/10.1007/s00702-022-02481-w.

Hagen, Lisa. "'Sex Addiction' Cited as Spurring Spa Shooting, But Most Killed Were of Asian Descent." NPR.org, 17 March 2021.

Heilman, Brian, Gary Barker, and Alexander Harrison. 2017. *The Man Box: A Study on Being a Young Man in the US, UK, and Mexico.* Promundo-US and Unilever.

Jha, Sonora. 2021. *How to Raise a Feminist Son: Motherhood, Masculinity, and the Making of My Family.* Sasquatch Books.

Orenstein, Peggy. *Boys & Sex Young Men on Hookups, Love, Porn, Consent, and Navigating the New Masculinity.* Harper, 2020: p.88.

Pinkett, Matt, and Mark Roberts. 2019. *Boys Don't Try? Rethinking Masculinity in Schools.* Routledge.

Rogers, Adam, Matthew Nielson, and Carlos Santos. 2021. "Manning Up While Growing Up: A Developmental-Contextual Perspective on Masculine Gender-Role Socialization in Adolescence." *Psychology of Men & Masculinity* 22(2): 354–364. https://doi.org/10.1037/men0000296.

Rosen, Nicole L., and Stacey Nofziger. 2019. "Boys, Bullying, and Gender Roles: How Hegemonic Masculinity Shapes Bullying Behavior." *Gender Issues* 36(3): 295–318. https://doi.org/10.1007/s12147-018-9226-0.

Zimbardo, Philip, and Nikita D. Coulombe. 2015. *Man Disconnected: How Technology Has Sabotaged What It Means to be Male*. Random House.

www.ingramcontent.com/pod-product-compliance
Lightning Source LLC
Chambersburg PA
CBHW071727120626
46550CB00002B/410